The Martyr's Son

The
Martyr's Son

✝

Armen John Arakelian,
Lori Ciccanti and Parease Arakelian,
with Cheryl Sasai Ellicott

Sweetwater Still Publishing
Colcord, Oklahoma

Visit Sweetwater Still Publishing at:

www.sweetwaterstill.com

All scripture quotations are taken from the 1769 King James Version of the Holy Bible (also known as the Authorized Version).

ISBN: 978-0-9843599-3-6
LCCN: 2016933103

Published by
Sweetwater Still Publishing
Colcord, Oklahoma

Printed in the United States of America

*Based on the true story of Armenian orphan
and genocide survivor, Armen John Arakelian.*

"Be sober, be vigilant; because your adversary the devil, as a roaring lion, walketh about, seeking whom he may devour . . ."

1 Peter 5:8

Table of Contents

From the Authors:

In the mid 1930s Armen Arakelian dictated his life story to writer Estelle Grant. It was published in 1935 as *Under a New Banner*, and in 1966 within the book *The False Prophet of Mecca*.

Unfortunately, not every character in this story left behind such detailed written memoirs. Therefore we've relied upon careful research, family tradition, and, where necessary, cautious speculation to bring certain scenes back to life—to the best of our ability.

We hope you enjoy Armen's story. We pray it impacts you as it has us.

Prologue

I
n the year 1853, an eleven-year-old boy kneeled to pray inside a little stone cottage, at the foot of Mount Ararat—the final resting place of the ark of the Bible.

"The God of Abraham, Isaac, and Jacob is calling me to pray, to fast, and to wait for an answer," he told his family. The boy, Efim Klubniken, bowed his head and began to wait. He wouldn't sleep, nor would he eat until he'd heard from God.

While the sun passed through the sky, the Klubniken family wondered if God would speak to little Efim. The boy had gone on prayer-vigils before, so they weren't surprised—only curious and expectant. Meanwhile, in the small village of Kara Kala, in the very heart of Armenia, their neighbors went about their business. The villagers were mostly Presbyterian or Orthodox Armenians. They shared a Christian faith, but not the extreme beliefs of the Russian-born Klubniken family. They agreed that a sleep-deprived, starved boy might hear voices, but they doubted it would be the voice of God!

Yet before a day had passed, Efim announced that God had replied with a message.

"What is the message?!" his anxious family asked.

"I don't know," Efim replied, appearing to stare at something invisible.

His relatives looked at one another, and then at Efim in confusion.

"The Almighty is speaking, but I cannot understand," Efim clarified.

What was this? The boy believed God spoke to him, but he didn't know what their Lord had actually said? Perhaps they should make him eat and lie down—after all, he was just a boy.

But Efim persisted. "I see a vision of charts," he said, "and a message in beautiful handwriting. If I had something to write upon, I might copy it down." Efim rose from his knees and went to the family's table. "Will you bring me paper and pen?"

Again his relatives were perplexed. Like many others in the region, the Klubniken family were not educated. Efim had never been to school. He could not read or write. It made no sense, nor was it easy to find what the boy requested.

But at last, a pen and blank paper were brought to him.

For the next seven days, Efim sat at the rough plank-table, staring at something only he could see. He was silent, except for the *scritch, scratch, scritch, scratch* of his pen upon the paper. Efim didn't eat; he didn't sleep. Stroke after careful stroke, he copied the shape of letters and diagrams that passed before his eyes.

At the end of seven days, Efim plunked down his pen, blinked a number of times, and gazed around at his eager family. His relatives exchanged nervous glances as they stared at the transformed pages; they were now nearly covered in lines, forms, and other marks.

"What is it, boy?" someone finally asked. Efim's writing was pretty, but it meant nothing to them.

Efim shrugged. "I don't know, for I cannot read it," he replied.

The family elders discussed the problem. A few of their neighbors could read. Should they show the pages to them? But what might their neighbors think? After all, Efim was completely unschooled. To expect he'd actually written a message, an announcement from the Almighty, no less, would be foolish. Kara Kala was a small village . . . senseless behavior was never forgotten. Nevertheless, the Klubnikens were people of great faith. Should they limit God by saying He couldn't give a written message to an illiterate boy?! At last they decided to walk by faith; they would take the pages to their neighbors who could read. But first, the women insisted, it was time for Efim to eat something.

As it turned out, Efim had written a totally legible message, in perfectly formed Russian letters—and it claimed to be a warning from God! The message declared that great danger was coming to the Christians in Kara Kala and beyond. Hundreds of thousands of men, women, and children would be brutally murdered, unless they left their homeland.

Leave their homeland? The Klubnikens and their neighbors listened to the message in wonder, until it proclaimed they must flee. Then they erupted with questions and doubts. How could this be? Were they really expected to leave their homes and livelihood because a young boy wrote that they should? How could hundreds of thousands of Christians be murdered, here, in this good and tranquil land?

Yet illiterate young Efim Klubniken had not only written a message in perfectly formed Russian letters, he had drawn maps showing exactly where the fleeing Christians were to go. When the time came, everyone in the region was to flee to a land far away, across the ocean. The maps amazed the educated villagers. This boy had never seen a geography book, but the body of water he drew so accurately was not the nearby Black Sea, nor the Caspian Sea. It wasn't even the farther-off Mediterranean. Efim had drawn an accurate map of the very distant Atlantic Ocean! At its shore, he drew a precise map of the United States of America.

But, the message said, the refugees were not to settle on the eastern side of this new land. They were to travel until they reached the west coast. There God would bless them, and their descendents would be a blessing to the nations. They were to stay there for many, many years, until a time of great persecution threatened that land as well—and at that time, the faithful remnant would again be told where to go.

Villagers were astonished, puzzled, and overwhelmed. They had listened to the message intently from beginning to end. Then, during the following weeks and months, they thought about it, they talked about it, they prayed about it, and they even told visitors who passed through Kara Kala about it. It was the most sensational event of their time.

Eventually, each person had to decide what they believed. Was Efim's message really from God, or not? The Bible said to beware of false miracles. They were warned that trusting emotional experiences opened a person up to believing almost anything. In the end, given these truths, most villagers doubted that Efim's message was true. There was undoubtedly a natural explanation for the *miraculous* writing. They just weren't sure what it was.

Those few who did believe in Efim's writings were considered emotional and experiential. In time these Efim-following, miracle-chasers no longer attended the churches where they'd once belonged. Instead, they joined with the few others who were like-minded.

Peaceful years followed in the region of Mount Ararat. In fact, decades passed, and still there was no slaughter. Efim grew to be a man, and many people called him a fraud. Efim, and those who believed his message, reminded their neighbors that the prophecies in the Bible often came dozens, or even hundreds of years before the event happened. The villagers replied, "Yes, but they came through *prophets*. God stopped giving men spiritual gifts after the Bible was complete!"

Many people called Efim *the Boy Prophet*, although he wasn't a boy anymore, and they didn't believe he was a prophet. Nevertheless, as the years passed, trouble between the Moslem Turks and the Christian Armenians increased. The hills around Ararat remained peaceful, but news of political troubles frequently reached the village. Each time they heard these reports, believers in Efim's message would get out the old pages and read them again. Then in August of 1896, a Turkish mob murdered more than six-thousand Armenians on the streets of Constantinople. The city of Constantinople was far away, but again Efim's followers prayed, "Lord, is it now time?" Year after year a few people continued to trust in the prophecy of Efim, but year after year, they said God wasn't telling them to flee just yet.

But at last, in the year 1900, Efim began to announce, "The time is near! We must now flee to America. All who remain here will perish!" It had been forty-seven years since he received this prophecy. He and others took out the now-yellowed pages and studied them intently. Then, while their neighbors looked on, Efim and his family packed.

Once again, Efim became the most-talked-about person in the region. Would he really leave home and take his family to an unknown land? A land where they would be homeless foreigners, all because he feared an imagined danger may come? Did Efim not realize that every nation, including America, was filled with real danger?

As the people of Kara Kala watched, Efim continued to pack. At last he and his little family got into their wagon, rolled out of the village, and out of sight. After he was gone, a few other Russian and Armenian families from Kara Kala followed in this modern-day exodus. In the months that followed, fear of this unseen, coming danger spread throughout the region. Over two-thousand families packed what they could take and abandoned the rest—including the beautiful lands that had been their homes for as long as they could remember.

But as each family left Armenia, those who stayed shook their heads in dismay. Who runs from an imaginary danger, to a place known to hold real danger? This didn't look like faith, but fear and foolishness. They had known of other groups that had followed so-called prophets to their destruction. Efim's old neighbors knew there weren't any truly safe places in the world. But most of all, they knew that God did not issue pinpoint instructions for modern people in a modern age.

By the year 1912, the last of the small group who followed the Boy Prophet had left for America.

"Jesus said unto them,
'If God were your Father,
ye would love me:
for I proceeded forth
and came from God;
neither came I of myself,
but he sent me.

Ye are of your father the devil,
and the lusts of your
father ye will do.

He was a murderer from the beginning,
and abode not in the truth, because
there is no truth in him.
When he speaketh a lie,
he speaketh of his own:
for he is a liar, and
the father of it."

John 8:42, 44

ONE

Zartar

July, 1914
Syrian Desert

". . . they wandered in deserts, and in mountains, and in dens and caves of the earth." Hebrews 11:38

The last of the Bedawee warriors disappeared over the highest sand dune just after midnight. When Zartar could no longer see the men, or hear the galloping and snorting of their Arabian horses, she silently lifted herself from the carpets. Quietly, and quickly, she gathered a few supplies and tied them inside a large cloth, making a bundle she could carry. Careful to stay in the shadows of the tents, she crept away from the warrior's fire, tiptoeing past where other women tended fires. Tonight there would be more victims; nonetheless, Zartar was glad the Bedawee men often went raiding at night. These were her only moments of relief and the only chance to hide her actions.

After clearing the edge of the Bedawee's temporary campsite, she broke into a sprint across the sand. Her legs, once plump and smooth like that of a cherished daughter, were now lean and strong like her Bedawee master's battle-scarred stallion. The full moon lit her way as she ran swiftly. If she were to stay alive, she must return before the warriors did.

Zartar was an Armenian from southeastern Turkey. Her family lived in the port city of Durtiol, near the eastern-most point of the Mediterranean coast. Five years earlier, when she was just fifteen-years-old, she was kidnapped by the Moslem Turks. The Turks sold her to the Arabs for fifteen Lira, which was less than the price of a camel. Then one day, while her Arab master's caravan was traveling southwest across the Syrian Desert, a group of nomadic Bedawee warriors attacked them. They slaughtered all of the Arab men, and Zartar was captured by a wild-eyed Bedawee warrior.

Every day her cruel Bedawee master painted a new tattoo on her delicate face, until it was completely covered. His tattoo marks declared that she was *his* property. But she knew differently. Zartar was a Christian; her real Master was the Lord Jesus Christ.

Zartar's small feet continued to pound the desert sand as she ran. Her long, thick braids swung at her sides and her robe billowed in the wind behind her. Eventually, she grew tired and her legs slowed, though her heartbeat continued to race. Her breath came in loud pants as she crossed the last place where the Bedawee warriors had butchered a vast crowd of Armenians—mostly women and children. As usual, after the slaughter, the Bedawees sent Zartar and the other captive-women out to strip the bodies of clothing and valuables.

Zartar ran on, almost numb to the horror that littered the desert around her. Memories of life before she was surrounded by misery and death were very faint. At last, when she was almost too winded to continue, Zartar reached a small, rocky ridge beside a crop of palm trees.

Panting, she rushed past the trees and climbed up the boulders to a small cave. When she reached the cave, she pulled a candle from the small bundle she carried. Lighting the candle, she entered the cave and hurried to the back. There she found a wounded teenage boy lying still on a soft bed of ferns — right where she'd left him.

"Are you better?" she asked, with a mixture of excitement and worry.

She knelt on the ground beside him, hoping he would respond. But just as the day before, there was no answer. Bowing her head, Zartar waited to catch her breath. At last she prayed aloud, "Master Jesus, You have finally let me find one of my people still alive! Will You now let this one die too?" Lifting her head and opening her eyes, Zartar watched the steady rise and fall of the boy's chest. Though still unconscious, his breathing was constant and strong. Zartar gazed at his face while the candlelight flickered and danced around the cave. The features of his pale face were striking.

"Please, my Lord and my God, let him live," she whispered.

Zartar was now twenty-years-old; she'd been a captive for five long, desolate years. She guessed this boy was about the age of her youngest brother, which would make him thirteen or fourteen. When Zartar was stolen, her baby brother hadn't even started school yet. Nursing this stranger might be the closest Zartar would ever come to seeing her beloved family again. Finding this boy alive held great significance . . . God had answered her prayers! The Almighty God of Abraham, Isaac and Jacob had chosen to save this one, out of so many. Surely this boy was destined for something important.

As she examined his peaceful face, she imagined he made his father proud and his mother laugh. She also imagined he had a sister who delighted in him. He reminded her very much of her baby brother, with his fair skin, dark hair and thick eyelashes. The boy's jaw-line was square and his chin strong; he would be a handsome man, like her older brothers and her father. Long-lost feelings filled Zartar as she stared at the teenage boy. Violence and death filled their land; did any of her family still live? Emotions she thought she no longer possessed washed over her. But as Zartar gazed through tear-filled eyes at the boy, she also felt a glimmer of hope.

Again she whispered, "Please, my God, give this boy a future . . . Please, God, give me a purpose and a reason to live."

Taking a goat-skin filled with water from her bundle, she dripped water into the unconscious boy's mouth. Wetting the edge of her robe she washed his cheeks and forehead.

Then she changed the cloth bandage on the oozing gash across his neck. That done, she bowed her head again. Zartar had prayed for this boy since she found him unconscious, held tightly in the arms of another Armenian teen—a young man that her Bedawee master had reduced to just a headless body.

At last Zartar stood to her feet. She wanted to stay longer, but fear and urgency were growing too strong. It was time to hurry back to the camp before she was missed.

"I'll return tomorrow night," she promised the boy. "I pray to my beloved Master in Heaven that you will awake."

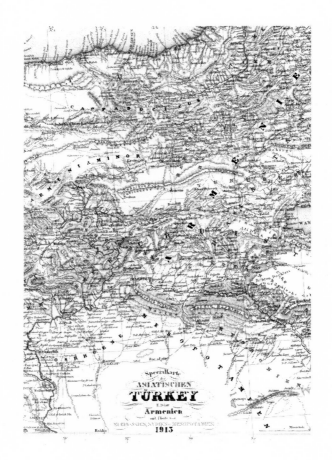

Specialkarte
der
ASIATISCHEN
TÜRKEY
II. Blatt
Armenien
und Theile von
KLEIN-ASIEN, SYRIEN, MESOPOTAMIEN
1915

two

Agayne

April, 1914; three months earlier
Nevsher, Turkey

"If the world hate you, ye know that it hated Me before it hated you." John 15:18

When dusk fled and the thickness of night settled over Nevsher, Agayne mourned the evil of the day. She lay on the floor by the church's back wall, where her son Armen had led her after the soldiers tore her wailing daughter from her arms. Her beautiful Parease . . . Agayne was beaten and bruised; the soldiers proved too strong for even her fiercest mother-love. So she had screamed aloud, begging her God for a miracle.

No miracle came; the Turks carried her innocent daughter away.

Emptied of tears at last, Agayne now lie still, inside a church that had been her place of joy. Many years earlier, she married her beloved Hagop here. Agayne wasn't much older than Parease when she fell in love with young Hagop. Dear, sweet Hagop . . . He had grown to be a devoted father and a gentle, loving husband. To this peaceful church Agayne and her good man brought their babies, one by one, and dedicated them to God. Their friends and neighbors cheered and embraced them. Their five precious boys and beautiful little girl Parease had grown up as members of this church-family. These same friends, relatives and neighbors were all gathered here now, mourning the events of the day.

Agayne moaned as a richer darkness shook her, seeping into the corners and filling the sanctuary. The black of night brought a temporary end to the Turkish revelry in blood, but the suffering of her priceless ones played on and on in Agayne's heart and mind. She wasn't prepared for such cruelty and bitterness. Things had been too good . . . before. Life was sweet, her family was happy. Oh, that such joy and tranquility could be swallowed in an instant! How was it possible? Today she had lost lovely Parease, dear Hagop and her three oldest boys—who had grown to be admirable young men . . . Agayne's pain was too great to bear.

Just two weeks ago the church bells were ringing as usual. Agayne's family had been whole and blessed. The Turkish town of Nevsher was home to an Armenian community with close ties. The Arakelian residence (and that of their relatives) was located on Arakel Street. Their church was just down the street; they could hear the bells from their home. On that morning Agayne and Hagop's youngest boys, Armen and Hoannes, were anxious to sing in the youth choir. The young teenage boys ran on ahead while their parents and sister Parease followed. Agayne held her husband's arm and patted his hand as they walked. His worry was unspoken, but Agayne knew. She wished for him to give these worries to their savior, but she certainly didn't blame him for his fear. Their lives under the Sultan's rule had been difficult, but now that the Young Turks had political power, the Arakelians and their fellow Armenians were truly worried. Yet when the church bells rang, Agayne could almost believe things were well.

Nonetheless, inside the beautiful stone church, the atmosphere was tense. All was not well. There would be no youth choir this day. Their Pastor, Dir Soruan, stood before them with tears streaming down his kind face.

"My friends," he said, "we are facing the greatest crisis ever met by the Christian church. I have a notice here that was placed in my hands by the Turkish guards. I will read it:

> 'By order of his most gracious Excellency the Sultan, this church is hereby ordered to disband and not reorganize except in the name of Mohammed. This is a final notice, and if it is not recognized within twenty days, the building will be burned and all of the people destroyed.'"

For Agayne, this read like a death sentence. She knew her beloved Hagop. While some might think they could just worship God in their secret place, Hagop would consider that a betrayal of his own conscience and a denial of his faith. Their neighbors would also refuse to comply with the Sultan's demand. They would rather die, and see their families die, than to deny their faith. Agayne's knees went weak at this thought.

The Arakelians were Armenians, yet they lived in the predominantly Moslem country of Turkey, which was part of the Ottoman Empire. For centuries the Ottoman Turks had conquered throughout the Mediterranean, Middle East, Eastern Europe, Spain and North Africa, carrying tens of thousands of people into slavery.

But early in the 1800s, the Turkish Ottoman Empire began to decline as the European countries of Greece, Serbia, Bulgaria and Romania won their independence. Armenia's geographical position made it a doorway between Europe and Asia, therefore, many Sultans considered Armenia *a danger spot.* To make matters much worse, Armenians embraced Christianity; this identified them more with *Christian Europe* than with *Pagan Asia.* In the late 1800s, when rumor said the Armenians wanted their independence, Sultan Abdul Hamid—known as *the Red Sultan*—responded fiercely by massacring one-hundred-thousand Armenian men, women and children.

After the Red Sultan was deposed in 1908, there was a brief euphoria and great hope among Armenians. Hope quickly dissolved after the government was taken over by *the Young Turks,* led by the three pashas (leaders) Mehmed Talaat, Ismail Enver and Ahmed Djemal. Although they seemed mild at the outset, their brutal ways were soon revealed.

Agayne stood quietly beside her husband, gripping his steady arm, while the crowd discussed the current political threats and the pastor answered their questions. Young Parease came to press up against her mother as the heated discussions swirled about them. Placing her arm around her trembling daughter, Agayne pulled her close and whispered words of comfort. Though she could be mischievous, Parease was Agayne's most sensitive child.

Life had never been entirely easy for the Armenians; the hatred between the Moslem Turks and the Christian Armenians was deep and bitter. But the recent assassination (in Serbia) of the heir to Austria-Hungary's throne, Archduke Franz Ferdinand, had set off a full-scale European war. Now the Central Powers (Germany, Austria-Hungary and the Ottoman Empire) were uniting against the Allied Powers of Britain, France, Russia and other smaller countries—countries identified as Christian.

It had the makings of a great war; Agayne and her husband Hagop feared that their people, and family, would be caught in the middle.

When the pastor finished speaking with his flock, the families silently slipped back out of the church and through the streets toward their homes.

Nevsher quickly began to look deserted. Businessmen closed their shops, schools shut down and young children could not be seen playing outside. Instead, the Armenian families gathered in their homes to pray.

Nine days later, in the stillness of the afternoon, the church bells broke forth in brisk, clanging notes. Louder and louder rang their frantic call. The bells were signaling a call for everyone to assemble in the Armenian church.

When they arrived, Dir Soruan was in the pulpit, waiting. The look on his face sent shivers down Agayne's body, freezing any bit of hope she retained. Pastor Dir Soruan was holding another paper. When the families were fully assembled, he read:

"In revision to his previous order, the Sultan will allow only five more days for the compliance of his wishes."

A greater silence filled the room as the congregation gazed at their Pastor for direction. After a pause, he spoke firmly, "Dear friends, it is useless for us to think there is any way possible to evade the trouble we face. Our turn has come; the Sultan means business. He will carry out his declaration. The one and only decision for us to make is this: are we going to meet this demand as Jesus Christ would meet it? Or are we going to renounce our faith and bow the knee to Mohammed?"

The people answered, "We will not bow down to Mohammed—Christ died for us, and we are ready to die for Him!" All around the church, heads nodded. Agayne's neighbors and relatives rose to their feet to show their resolve. In the front row, a young man cried out, "If need be, we will fight to the end for our God!" Around the room other men echoed his words.

Dir Soruan motioned for quiet, then turned toward a picture of Christ hanging in the front of the altar. Bowing his head, he prayed aloud, "Oh Lord Jesus, give us strength, give us power, give us faith to honor and obey Thee! If it be Thy will, turn these terrible people aside from their purpose—if not; prepare us to meet them according to Thy will. In the Name of our Christ, we ask it, amen."

After this news, many families were afraid to go home. Others intended to fight the soldiers; they declared that the stone church was a better fortress, especially for un-armed men. Military service was not permitted for the Armenians. They were heavily taxed for this *freedom from military service*, but it was not negotiable; their Turkish leaders considered it too dangerous to allow Armenians the art of using weapons.

However, still others implored the group to meet the violence with non-resistance.

"Friends, please listen," they begged, "we're not being asked to deny our Christ. We are only banned from assembling in this building! We must respond in love, prayer and forgiveness," they said, "just as our Lord and Savior Jesus Christ met his enemies."

In the end, the majority decided that the people should all stay together in the church—the building they were ordered to vacate. And so, the waiting began. Mothers embraced their children, while the men inclined toward physical resistance took charge guarding the doors and windows. Together the group suffered hunger as the sleepless hours ticked slowly away. Only the eyes of the terrified friends, neighbors and relatives seemed alive, burning and boring through the hours in a ceaseless effort to read the future. Long, nightmarish days passed, and then, suddenly, that for which they waited came.

On the morning of the fifth day, the weary group were startled by the sound of soldiers ascending the church steps. A squad of formidable Turkish soldiers, headed by a captain resplendent in his jeweled fez, gold braid, curved saber and clanking spurs, mounted the church steps noisily and pounded on the door, shouting:

"Open the door in the name of the Sultan!"

The men at the front of the church shouted back, "We do not recognize the Sultan!"

"If you do not open, we will break down the door," the soldiers replied. "This is your last chance—will you open?"

"We will not—if you want us, you will have to fight your way in," shouted one of the Armenian men in response.

Without further parley, the door was battered, split and ripped from its hinges; heavily-armed Turkish soldiers swarmed into the church over the splintered door. Armenian women and children cowered in the shadows, while their unarmed, defenseless men stood between them and the imminent threat. The men stood motionless, despite the rifles aimed at them.

Then, with unconscious dramatic force and power, their beloved pastor forced his way through the crowd and faced the captain. Agayne looked on, grieved, noting the simple, quiet dignity that clothed Dir Soruan like a mantle. With the gentle simplicity of a child, he spoke:

"Please don't kill these men. It is I whom you want, not they. I am ready to go—take me."

It seemed that an unwilling gleam of admiration leapt up in the captain's eyes, even as he caught the old man by the shoulder, shaking him unmercifully. At this indignity, the men sprang forward to protect their leader, but were pushed back into the shadows by bayonets and fists of the soldiers, while the captain addressed Dir Soruan.

"You do not seem to understand that the Sultan's order is law and must be obeyed," he said.

"God's orders come before those of the Sultan," Dir Soru-an answered quietly.

At that, the captain turned and ordered his soldiers, "Throw him down the steps!"

Hiding in the shadows of her husband and their three grown boys, Agayne pulled her young teenage boys to her side and held her quaking daughter. As their pastor hurled down the many steps, Parease whimpered and pressed her eyes tightly against her mother's shoulder. When the pastor lay broken upon the street below, the soldiers tied him with a rope and dragged him away.

After Dir Soruan was gone, the captain turned to the guards and repeated the orders he'd received from the governor: "Kill all the men and boys who are able to hold a gun!" he shouted.

"Hang them, shoot them, or cut off their heads," he continued, "but kill them all. Then loot the town and burn their homes!" Before noon, about eighteen hundred men had lost their lives, including Agayne's dear, sweet Hagop and their three grown boys.

When the soldiers tore the men away from their families, they ignored thirteen-year-old Armen, thinking him a child. However, at fifteen, his brother Hoannes could certainly hold a gun. But, by a miracle, when the men were all gone, Hoannes still remained. Throughout the rest of the day Hoannes attempted to keep out of sight, and Agayne held Parease and Armen tightly, mourning the loss of her husband and three of her sons. She prayed that God would shield her remaining children. Yet before the sun had set, as one gathers flowers from a trampled garden, the soldiers came for the girls and young women. Agayne knew well what awaited her innocent little girl, Parease, yet she was powerless; the soldiers violently ripped her daughter from her protective arms. Yet once again, Agayne's two youngest boys remained. For the moment, Agayne was still a mother.

As she now lie weeping for those lost, Agayne heard a silent whisper, again and again, urging her to remember her boys. Urging her to respond to her responsibilities as a mother . . . *Rise up, Agayne. Rise up* . . . She had lost so much. Nevertheless, Armen and Hoannes needed their mother. *Rise up, Agayne. Rise up* . . . For them Agayne dared not surrender to the emotions that threatened to envelope her now. *Rise up . . . Rise up* . . .

In the faint moonlight Agayne saw others huddled inside their dear church, some moaning and sobbing, but many were silent, slumped down, staring into the black of the night. Near the front doors were the silhouettes of many Turkish guards. When the light of day returned, they would surely continue their slaughter. At her side was little Armen, slumped over like so many others, silent, staring at nothing . . . waiting to die.

Rise up, Agayne!

Today Armen watched his beloved father and his three oldest brothers die. He watched his sister Parease torn from his mother's arms to be sold into a harem. Now, it seemed, Armen was watching his mother give up all hope . . . Finally, touched by the posture of her son, Agayne began to pray silently. *Oh, my precious Lord. How can I rise up? I am nothing. Rise up to what? I have nothing left. I have nothing to give. Oh, my Lord! Be my strength.* The minutes ticked by and Agayne continued to pray, begging for strength. As she prayed, a plan began to unfold within her mind. *There just might be a way . . . she could see it . . . yes . . . she might save her boys.* They were under heavy guard, making this plan very dangerous. But if Agayne did nothing, they were already as good as dead. She might save her boys, if she would only rise up. At last Agayne lifted herself into a sitting position and leaned against the wall.

"Armen," she said at last, "where is your brother?"

"He is under the pew," the boy answered flatly.

"Hoannes, come," she whispered into the dark. Within seconds, Hoannes shuffled to her side and sunk down beside her. Praying silently again, she thanked God for the strength of the mother-love she felt awakening within her. The Lord was answering her prayers; only this could enable her to retain her sanity.

Splitting the blackness, the dim moonlight shone through the tall windows. Agayne laid her hand on her son's head, brought his ear close to her lips and whispered, "Tonight, Hoannes, when it's darkest, you must try to get out of here. Can you squeeze through one of the cellar windows?"

"Maybe; I'll try anyhow," Hoannes replied quietly.

"I believe you and Armen will have a better chance to escape dressed as old women. After you get out, gather up enough clothes to disguise yourselves, and then come back and stay close beside me."

"I'll do my best, Mother," promised Hoannes.

"Go, and may God protect you," she said. Not much later, Agayne listened to the faint sounds she alone could interpret as Hoannes tiptoed down the dark staircase and wriggled through a tiny basement window below.

Three

Armen

"For I am persuaded, that neither death, nor life, nor angels, nor principalities, nor powers, nor things present, nor things to come, nor height, nor depth, nor any other creature, shall be able to separate us from the love of God, which is in Christ Jesus our Lord." Romans 8:38-39

Hoannes made it back to the church just before daybreak. Armen hadn't realized he slept, until the hushed tones of his mother and older brother woke him. "Quick, Armen," his mother whispered, "I must get you into this clothing before daylight."

At thirteen years of age, Armen had always enjoyed a comfortable home, the love of good parents and happy companionship of sister and brothers. His home was a secure haven of orderliness and beauty, furnished in the traditional, sumptuous Oriental manner. Intricately engraved low, silver tables were surrounded by floor mats, the coffee mill and the goat-skin refrigerator. He could not have visualized any danger from which his father or mother would not be able to protect and save their family. To be sure, faint war clouds had dimmed Europe's horizon, but Armen had not thought to worry; he lived in the peaceful village of Nevsher, where nothing very exciting ever happened. From babyhood, every Armenian child understood that the Turks hated them; their chief desire was to destroy them. Well, to be frank, Armen and his friends and relatives had no love for the Turks either.

But as a boy of thirteen, Armen had no real concept of hatred, worry or danger. Only recently the responsibility of baking the bread (lavash) over an earthenware utensil had been given to him. That he was finally trusted to bake Armenian flat bread, which his family used as a utensil to eat their food, filled him with a great sense of maturity. Such was his uncomplicated life. However, as the first rays of light filtered through the windows of the grand stone church, Armen's eyes were opening to a reality he'd never imagined.

By the time the sun rose, Armen and his fifteen-year-old brother Hoannes looked much like the rest of the older women. But with the morning light, there came frantic cries all around them.

"Fire, Fire!" the people screamed.

Within moments great tongues of flame raged along the back wall of the church, leaping forward to lick the nearest row of pews. With the stampeding group, Armen ran toward the front door, stumbling over his new clothing. His mother and wide-eyed brother Hoannes were at his side. In the midst of the turmoil, Armen heard soldiers laughing outside. Of course the Turks had no concept of a human soul. To them a horse, camel or a dog was just as valuable as a human being—sometimes even more so.

Nevertheless, Armen wondered how even a Turk could find humor in this.

Tightly pressed inside the teeming, panicked crowd, Armen, Hoannes and Agayne moved forward, finally reaching the foyer, just inside the destroyed front door of the stone building. Suddenly, behind them, the church's roof fell with a mighty crash. All who remained in the building were buried. In front of Armen and his family, those near the front of the line screamed and rushed forth, seeking the safety of the street—only to be met by gunfire. Mothers, with their little boys and girls clutched in their arms, fell, then lay twisted and scattered across the blood-spattered church steps.

In the battered doorway at the top of the steps, women, children and a few elderly men cowered in relative safety. Except for the piercing wails of the very youngest of children, the group had gone completely silent; they were overcome by the thick smoke billowing out of the building behind, the frightful, crackling noise of the fire and the extreme horror on the steps before them. As the gunfire ceased, the sobbing cries of the babies were overshadowed by the ever-increasing roar and whoosh of the inferno as it consumed the church building and those trapped inside.

At last an order was heard above the noise: "March the rest of them to the courthouse!"

Armen, Hoannes and their mother were among the survivors who were crudely herded away from their burning church and down the deserted streets. Agayne and Hoannes alternately held Armen from falling when his feet tangled in his new skirt. "Armen," his mother whispered at last, "clutch the sides of the garment in your palms; lift the excess off the ground," she said. Continuing in that manner, Armen found walking easier.

The Turkish city of Nevsher had its Armenian section; here Armen had lived all of his thirteen years. His family worshipped the Lord Jesus and reached out for the finer things of life. Armen admired his hardworking, peaceful father and other Armenian businessmen like him. However, Armen had long-since developed a deep disdain for the lazy Turks. The Turkish men never worked. Instead, they kept from two or three, to eight wives; these they put to work while they spent their time in the coffee houses, hatching up mischief. The Turk's wicked treatment of their women was well-known and often discussed among the Armenians. A Turk's newest wife was the official head of household, and she always treated her husband with great love and respect, for she feared he would bring home a new wife, and then she would no longer be the head of the home. Instead, she would be sent to work in the fields with the less-important wives. According to Turkish custom, the wives had been purchased, the price being two or three horses, a couple of camels, or a certain amount of wheat and sometimes gold, therefore, they were the man's property to do with as he wished. And not only were the Turks wild, ruthless, uncivilized beasts who treated their women pitifully—they had no educational system, such as the Armenians enjoyed. In fact, there were so many points of difference between the

Turks and Armenians that there had never seemed the slightest chance of tearing down the wall of hatred which separated them. This hatred was so real and menacing that the Armenians had prepared underground passageways of refuge and sanctuary, against the day when this hatred would actually break bounds in an effort to consume them.

However, this had all been so much a part of Armen's daily life that he had accepted it much as one becomes accustomed to the shining of the sun and the patter of rain drops on the roof. It was all so close to him that he failed to get the proper perspective on it.

Until now.

When at last the battered group arrived at the courthouse, they looked up to see their pastor being drug onto the balcony. He was covered in blood. The governor stepped onto the balcony and took a stance above them. Pointing toward Pastor Dir Soruan, the governor addressed the crowd of horrified Armenian women, children and old men who stood cowed below.

"Do you see this dog?" he shouted. "You can save him and yourselves. This is your last chance!"

Armen glanced at his mother; she was silent and still, but fresh tears streamed down her lovely cheeks. Armen was immediately thankful that his dear mother looked old and worn to strangers. If they could see her true beauty, she too would have been stolen from him and sold into a

Turkish harem. Pressing closer, Armen grasped her hand tightly. Agayne squeezed back.

Above them the governor continued his speech: "What good is your God? Renounce Him. Accept Mohammed and you will go free!"

But the weary mothers only hugged their little ones tighter, wept and shook their heads firmly and unanimously. Armen's mother gazed around at her beloved companions, raised her trembling chin and cried out in a weak voice, "We can not!"

At this, the governor turned and, laughing, gave orders to the soldier nearest to Dir Soruan. Obeying, the solider turned and thrust a hot iron into the pastor's eyes. For the next few moments, the crowd endured the agonizing screams of their dear friend and minister, until his cries were abruptly ended by the sound of a gunshot.

Armen stared at the scene around him. First Papa, then his brothers and even their relatives, friends and neighbors. Now their pastor was dead. Armen had never imagined such horror.

In fact, the incidents of the past twenty-four hours were utterly incomprehensible.

four

Anneza

May, 1914
Everek, Turkey

If the voice of God in history speaks to us from age to age,
Then within the year now past us, while the Balkan war did rage,
He has surely been directing the attention of the church,
To the land of Asia Minor, that is waiting for research.

Here the Turk, the Kurd, the Arab, Greek, Armenian and Jew,
With the Syrian, Circassian and Albanian wait for you;
All so needy of the Gospel, in this Moslem land so drear.
Will you help to send The Message that will lift their lives, and
cheer?

Suffering and destitution stalk abroad throughout the land;
Cries of sorrow, pain and anguish can be heard on every hand.
Soldiers, to the front in numbers, went, — Alas! ne'er to return,
Leaving sobbing wives and children, all alone their bread to earn.

Is the church of Christ content, that while this war did thus afford
Contact with the Moslem peoples-it be only of the sword?
Let us rather show the spirit of the One on Calvary,
He, whose symbol is the cross and, who loves all humanity.

- Mrs. D. C. Eby, Hadjin and Everek Orphanages

After spending hours gathering wild roka in the hot sun, Anneza was tired. Exceedingly tired. Nearby, under the only shade tree, her baby sister Serapi slept in a basket. On the rocky slope beside her, Anneza's mother, Vartuhi Ohanian, stopped to rest. Thankful for the break, Anneza took the moment to also sit upon a flat stone.

After a few minutes, her mother rose, slowly walked to where Serapi slept and gathered the basket into her arms. Looking back at her oldest daughter, Vartuhi's voice was weak as she spoke, "Anneza, I think we have enough for a few days," she said. "Take the rudsack while I carry your sister."

Anneza dreaded the long, arduous walk down the rocky hillside, but she knew not to complain. Lifting the bag of wild, bitter greens onto her back, Anneza took her mother's arm, and they began their journey home. The Ohanians lived at the foot of Mount Argeus, in the Armenian district of the village of Everek, in southeastern Turkey.

At twelve-years-old, Anneza Ohanian knew better than to complain about small things like weariness, hunger, or eating wild roka night after night. Some months earlier Anneza's father was conscripted into the Turkish army; every day since then Anneza, and her mother and brothers, waited for word of him. Day after long day passed, and no word came.

In the meantime, life grew more difficult. Anneza's teenage brothers, Garabed (named after his father), Vartan and Kircor, were trying hard to run their father's barber shop, but there was very little business. There was also a food shortage in their region, made even worse when the Ottoman soldiers helped themselves to whatever they wanted. Fortunately, they had left behind the Ohanian family's goat and a few scattered potatoes—for now.

At last Anneza and her mother reached the bottom of the rocky slope and walked alongside the high stone wall that surrounded a two-acre field of flowers; behind the wall, a foreign missionary society was building an orphanage. For the past year or more, Anneza had walked this path with her mother, watching the orphaned boys hard at work on the wall that would surround their new home. Anneza knew many of the one-hundred and twenty boys by name; they were currently housed in seven private homes throughout her neighborhood. For lack of a safer place, those who weren't old enough to help build spent their days playing in the streets.

Anneza loved to watch the boys work; each time she passed by the wall was a little longer, or a little taller. And now their high wall was finally finished! All of the Everek orphan boys, except the smallest, had carried sand and stone to erect the indispensable stone wall.

More than anything, Anneza loved the times when she and Mother passed by and heard the boys singing. As the months since her Father left drew longer, those moments grew more precious. To see these boys, who had no families, smiling and singing of God's love encouraged Anneza's fretful heart.

As Anneza and her mother approached the front gate, boys of all sizes shouted greetings and waved from below, beside and even atop the wall. "Hoshgelden! Hoshgelden!" they cried out in the common language of the land—meaning "you have come pleasantly," or "we welcome you!" Many times Anneza had wished to shout out a reply, but she just couldn't do it. Instead, she caught her bottom lip between her teeth and felt heat rush into her face.

Near the enormous gate sat one of the missionaries, just inside the wall, at a small table, under a canopy. When they drew near, she looked up from writing in her journal and waved. "Mrs. Ohanian, come and join me!" she called out pleasantly. Motioning to chairs in the shade of the canvas canopy, the missionary rose, took the heavy basket from Anneza's mother and hugged her warmly. "Vartuhi, I had hoped to see you today," she said. "We have food for you and your children. This evening Miss Lambert, Mrs. Eby and the older boys wish to deliver it to you."

Vartuhi Ohanian shook her head, but sunk slowly down into the proffered chair. "Oh, but I cannot accept," she said. "Not again, Katherine."

"Nonsense, Vartuhi," Katherine replied. Sitting, the pretty, young American missionary reached into the basket and lifted little Serapi into her arms. She held the wiggling infant close to her chest, shut her eyes, sighed and smiled. Opening her eyes, she placed a tender kiss on Serapi's forehead. "My dear friend, you know the mission board provides additional funds for widows." Katherine paused and cleared her throat. "And also for women whose husbands are away for an extended period," she finished.

"I don't wish to accept what I have not earned," Vartuhi replied.

"The Lord has provided for you, Vartuhi. For the sake of your children," the missionary said gently.

The two women stared at each other for a moment. At last, Vartuhi smiled wearily and nodded her head. "When my husband returns," Vartuhi said, "We will repay you."

"Until then," replied Katherine, "God will repay us."

Suddenly Katherine turned to Anneza, where she stood listening to the women talk and watching the boys scramble down from the wall to resume working. "Oh, Anneza! Please sit too! Come, rest. You have worked so hard helping your mother."

Anneza blushed, but she gladly accepted the chair. Katherine placed glasses in front of Anneza, and her mother, and poured water from a pitcher. Accepting the gift, Anneza gulped loudly, forgetting her manners in the midst of her thirst and exhaustion.

Afterward, long restful moments passed while Anneza reveled in the comfortable chair and the blessed shade, listening to her mother and the missionary talk of war and other things. From the corner of her eye, Anneza watched a few of the teenage boys as they passed back and forth through the gateway, moving load after load of sand and stone in the hot midday sun. As usual, the boys stole glances her way while she pretended not to notice. By now Anneza knew which boys carried much heavier loads when they thought she might be watching. She also knew that all boys were quite absurd—and some much more than others. Nevertheless, she did enjoy watching them work.

After a few moments, Serapi began to fuss in the missionary's lap; Anneza rose, took her baby sister into her arms and sat again, situating Serapi on her skirts to make a bit of a swing. Serapi relaxed, smiled and placed her tiny hand into her mouth as her older sister gently swung her back and forth.

With one eye secretly on the antics of the boys, Anneza quietly hummed one of the songs she'd learned passing by this place. On the table near her now-empty glass, a spotted butterfly landed beside the missionary's journal. The butterfly lifted into the air and flitted about, catching Serapi's attention; the baby followed it with her large, brown eyes, until they began to drift closed. Anneza rocked her gently, humming more quietly. Meanwhile, the wind continued to riffle the pages of the journal on the table; Anneza watched the pages and admired the woman's beautiful handwriting as the paper lifted and fell in the slight breeze. She hoped to have such lovely penmanship some day as well. Soon Serapi was sleeping again and Anneza felt her own eyes begin to grow heavy.

Of all the people in town, Anneza enjoyed the missionaries most. They also spoke of war and other frightening things, however, being in their presence made Anneza feel safer. These were God's special people, sent from around the world. Anneza noticed Vartuhi also was happier after her visits with the missionaries or when the Bible-women from the orphanage came to visit and read the Holy scriptures with her. It helped that they frequently brought food, usually just when the Ohanian family needed it most.

Although Anneza was only eight-years-old when the missionaries came to Everek, bringing over a hundred orphaned boys to live in her small village, she remembered. And she knew her people's history. In 1909, as part of the Young Turk Revolution, the Turks overran the town of Adana, burning over four-thousand Armenian homes. The outbreaks spread throughout the district and thirty-thousand Armenians were killed. Eleven hundred children were left without families. Because the nearby town of Hadjin was able to withstand the Turkish assault, Adana's orphans were first brought to Hadjin and its villages. Americans had built an orphanage in Hadjin a few years before Anneza was born. Then in 1910, the Barkers and Eby's, missionaries from Canada, expanded the orphanage by creating a boy's home here in Everek (several days journey by horseback from Hadjin). The girls remained at the orphanage station in Hadjin, and all of the boys were moved to Everek. The next year, the missionaries opened an orphan's school in Everek and also a school for the blind. They also held a weekly meeting for Protestant women; Anneza and her mother had visited twice.

Anneza wanted to attend again, but Vartuhi was too tired since Serapi's birth. Truth be told, it had also caused problems with their neighbors and relatives, most of whom were Gregorian—members of the Armenian Apostolic church.

Anneza's musings stopped suddenly as she heard her mother and the missionary discussing her.

"We know Anneza to be a gifted student," Katherine said. "If by chance you cannot afford the Gregorian school this coming year, we'd be pleased to have Anneza and your sons attend with us, free of tuition."

Vartuhi sighed and wiped at her forehead. "I may accept for the boys," she said, "but I need Anneza's help with the little babe just now."

"Oh, how I understand that," said Katherine. "What I wouldn't give to have Anneza's help myself!"

Anneza blushed and smiled, but remained silent. She had only occasionally been brave enough to speak to the missionaries—although she loved to hear them speak.

Katherine nodded. "Then again, you should know there are rumors that we'll be forced to leave the country."

"Leave?" Anneza blurted out, suddenly worried enough to find her tongue. "Whatever do you mean?"

"Just that," replied Katherine. "We are all either American or Canadian subjects. With Turkey at war with Great Britain, the likelihood of the Canadians being called home by their mission board is high. Likewise, it's doubtful whether Turkey will allow even we neutral Americans to stay."

"But you cannot leave!" Anneza said, startling her baby sister and even herself at her outspokenness. Serapi began to cry and chew her tiny fists. Vartuhi rose with great effort and lifted Serapi into her arms. She comforted the infant then situated her inside her basket, signaling that it was near time to leave for home.

"Anneza," Katherine replied, reaching across the table to pat her hand, "three-fourths of our present staff, of forty workers, were once our orphan boys and girls. They are now our teachers, stewards, cooks, bakers, Bible-women, seamstresses, tailors and carpenters. They will not be leaving; they're fully capable of caring for the boys in our absence."

"Yes, but what of the souls of the Armenians?" Anneza asked.

"What of their souls?" asked the missionary.

"You yourself said, 'Although the Armenians are known as a *Christian* nation, one is greatly impressed by the utter lack, among the majority, of a saving knowledge of the truth,'" Anneza answered.

Momentarily taken aback, Katherine paused, looking perplexed. At last she smiled and nodded, then reached forward, plucked her open journal from the table,and tucked
it into the carpet-bag at her feet.

"Dear, Anneza," she said, "we have two Bible-women at
this point—native Armenians who grew up in our homes.
Last year they visited hundreds of homes, held countless
meetings, handed out many Bibles and publications, and
yes, everywhere they found weary, hungry, tempted
hearts needing the strength of Jesus. There has recently
been an awakening among the Armenian/Gregorian
women here, with some receiving assurance of sins forgiven and others inquiring about the plan of salvation.
We have also received news of a revival in Adana. We do
not know just how many have been converted through
these efforts, as the record of souls is kept above, but fruit
has followed this ministry. I'm of a mind to believe that
God will continue His work whether or not we are here."

At this Vartuhi interrupted, "Anneza, the babe is hungry."

Rising with hesitance, Anneza shouldered the rudsack of
roka while her mother lifted Serapi's basket into her arms
and thanked the missionary for her hospitality.

"The women and boys will come to your home this evening with food," Katherine reminded her. Anneza and
Vartuhi then set off on the path toward home. Behind
them some of the boys clamored back atop the wall to
watch them go.

Anneza didn't want the missionaries to leave Everek. Fears flooded her heart and mind as she walked; the peace she'd felt earlier had evaporated entirely. It didn't matter that many of the orphanage workers were Armenians and would remain; the missionaries had to stay as well! Anneza knew her people's history well enough to know they were at the mercy of the Turks, unless Christian foreigners stepped in to defend them. Even Everek had been burned by the Turks just seven years before Anneza's birth. Who had stopped the massacres of non-Moslems under the rule of the Red Sultan? Foreigners! Who took in the orphans of Adana? Foreigners! These foreign missionaries had to stay and build the orphanage behind that strong wall, amidst the beautiful flowers of the field. So long as they had a wall—and American and Canadian missionaries—the fatherless children of Everek would be safe.

Despite the horrific past, Anneza wanted desperately to believe Armenians could live peacefully with their Moslem neighbors—without the help of peace-keeping foreigners. However, things looked grim; her hope grew dimmer each day that Father was gone. If the Turks would allow him to come home for a visit, or even to send word of his whereabouts and safety, then she might believe it.

Until then, she would not.

five

Armen

"I have told you these things, so that in Me you may have peace. In this world you will have trouble. But take heart! I have overcome the world." John 16:33

Life had become ugly and dreadful. From the Nevsher courthouse, the band of surviving women and children were herded on foot toward the Syrian Desert. Leaving the pillaged city, one more trial was given them to bear: they were compelled to pass close beside the *death carts* containing the massacred bodies of their husbands, fathers and brothers.

With eyes straight ahead, Agayne whispered to her sons, "They are now in Heaven enjoying God's presence. Look only ahead, march on and praise God that our loved ones have won the victory."

Armen diverted his eyes, but he could not so easily rid his mind of despair. *Why would a loving God allow them to suffer so for their faith and loyalty?*

Armen couldn't answer his own question, but he feared to hurt his mother with such doubts.

Two unforgettable weeks passed, and still they struggled on, enduring ruthlessness, unspeakable indignities and suffering. The group was given no food; at times they found a bit of dry grass along the wayside.

Each new day, as they continued to march, Armen watched friends, neighbors and relatives stumble, fall and die from lack of food, exhaustion and disease. Mile after painful mile, as his stomach gnawed with hunger, Armen listened to the words of his enemy taunting the struggling travelers:

"How is it your Christ does not come and help you? Call on Mohammed even now, and we will feed you!" they shouted.

Without fail, Armen's dear limping mother would squeeze his hand tightly and whisper words of encouragement in response. "Wasn't Jesus Himself taunted by the enemy when He encountered Satan in the wilderness?" she whispered. "Yet He overcame temptation by quoting the scriptures."

Armen loved his mother and wanted to agree with everything she said, but he was confused. At times, he wondered why Christ did not respond to their prayers.

At last his brother Hoannes voiced similar concerns. "But, Mother," Hoannes asked in hushed tones, "why hasn't Christ overcome the wickedness of the Turks yet? We quote the scriptures day and night, to no avail."

Mother reached up and stroked his gaunt cheek, then responded quietly, "Hoannes, our battle is not against flesh and blood."

"It certainly appears to be so," Hoannes replied, slowing his pace to give his mother a brief rest. "And we have been defeated."

Agayne smiled at her son as she leaned upon his arm. "Put on the whole armor of God," she quoted, "that ye may be able to stand against the wiles of the devil. For we wrestle not against flesh and blood, but against principalities, against powers, against the rulers of the darkness of this world, against spiritual wickedness in high places."

"But what is the armor of God?" asked Armen.

"The belt of truth, the breastplate of righteousness, the Gospel of peace, the shield of faith, the helmet of salvation and the sword of the Spirit," his brother Hoannes recited.

"Yes, the sword of the Spirit—which is the *Word of God*," Mother finished the verse. "With this sword we are victorious."

Hoannes shook his head wearily. "If our enemy is the devil, we've even less chance," he said. "Undoubtedly the devil is too powerful even for faithful Armenians."

"Nor can I imagine how to receive this armor," Armen remarked.

"No, my sons," Agayne said gently, "we are not defeated and *we do have our armor!* Do we not know the truth? Jesus Himself is the way, the truth and the life! Do we not posses righteousness? We are clothed in Christ's righteousness—thus, and only thus—we gain access to the Father, Almighty God. Moreover, we are His ambassadors of peace, through faith in the Gospel. Have we not forgiveness of our sins, and salvation, through the shed blood of our beloved Jesus? Yes! Then my sons, remain in God's armor—*remain in Christ*—wherein we have already overcome!"

Hoannes didn't appear entirely convinced, and truth be told, Armen was now more thoroughly confused. What had they overcome? Armenians, who had always worshipped the Lord Jesus, were being repaid for their faithfulness with cruelty and dishonor. This was their victory? As a rule, the Armenians, generation after generation, were fine, industrious, intelligent, business-like, honorable people. They hated that which God hates; they renounced the temptation of evil; they were not enticed toward the other side of Nevsher, where the wicked, lazy Turks worshipped Mohammed and reveled in their pagan ignorance. And hadn't God shown favor to these faithful Armenians before? Hadn't God blessed the Arakelians with peace and the finer things of life? Hadn't he previously seen their goodness and devotion—and loved them for it?

But now, after the vicious slaughter by the Turks, followed by two weeks of marching, very few Armenians of Nevsher remained. Now, in their current destitute and tormented state, Mother believed they had overcome their enemy? Mile after cruel mile, Armen set his mind to make sense of it, but he could not.

At last, those who survived the trek finally reached a Turkish military settlement, called Ulu Kerslaugh. Here they met thousands of Armenians, from other towns, just as weak and malnourished as they were. For dinner that first evening everyone was rationed a morsel of bread — it was the first ration they had received since their march began.

"Ah, it is like manna from heaven!" Armen declared. No one could understand how delicious a dry morsel of bread could taste unless they too had experienced real hunger.

After eating their portion, the Nevsher group was assigned to a little clearing and told to make camp. Here they were commanded to stay, under penalty of instant death. By feigning deafness, Armen and Hoannes were not required to speak when spoken to. Therefore, the soldiers, still fooled by the boys' disguise, allowed them to share a pavilion with their mother. With guards close by the tent, Armen's mother quietly led them in prayer, offering thanks and calling upon the Lord to lift them out of the depths of despair.

Days passed, and, while certainly the conditions were far from decent, the little family welcomed the rest. After just one week in the camp, their health improved somewhat, for they at least rested and had a bit more to eat than while on the march. Also, in this camp, as in all such plac-es, Arabic peddlers abounded, hoping to profit from the misfortune of the crowd. One night, after a supper of just the dry grass near their tent, Mother whispered to Armen in the dark, "Armen, wake up," she said, gently stroking her son's shoulder. "Where is Hoannes?!" she asked.

Armen shook his weary head and opened his eyes. "I don't know," he replied.

Hours passed while Armen worried and Mother prayed. Just before daybreak, when Armen had nearly given up hope, Hoannes crawled under the edge of the tent, clutch-ing a full loaf of bread in his hand. To his bewildered fam-ily, he explained: "I set about to track the peddlers down and filch enough food to keep hunger from being too troublesome for you."

After Mother calmed her tormented heart, Hoannes relat-ed the story of his evening. "I slipped out of the tent after dark, and I quickly found what I sought—an Arab ped-dler," Hoannes said with a sly smile. "To my great joy, he was sleeping! On a flat rock beside him, stood his basket. But handicapped by my feminine attire—and driven by the pangs of hunger—I threw caution to the wind. In my overeager approach, I managed to overturn his basket the moment I touched it."

Armen listened to his brother's tale with great interest, but he also noticed his mother shaking her head slowly back and forth; she had folded her hands in her lap and was muttering quietly under her breath.

"Wide awake in a moment," Hoannes said, "the Arab clutched me in a vise-like grip, and the tussle was on!"

At this, Armen found himself sitting forward, his eyes wide.

"And wouldn't you know it," Hoannes continued, "but the Arab promptly yelled for the soldiers! And myself, frightened to the point of desperation, I grabbed a good sized stone." Hoannes turned to his mother. "I am sorry, Mother. But I struck the Arab a blow on the head, which knocked him senseless." He shrugged. "It wasn't as if the fellow didn't deserve that and worse. I could hear the guards running toward us in answer to the peddler's cry."

Armen sat, altogether mesmerized—but frightened as well, at the retelling of his brother's adventure. Hoannes recounted how fear had poured over him like so much ice water. Clutching his skirts in anything but a lady-like manner, Hoannes had begun to run, but promptly stumbled and fell into a ditch.

"Immediately," Hoannes said, "I realized the ditch was a capital place in which to hide, so I lay very still, anxiously waiting to see what would happen. The soldiers passed close beside me to reach the Arab, who, by this time, was recovering from the blow I gave him. From the ditch, I listened as the Arab began to relate his story:

'I was attacked by an old woman!' the Arab shouted. 'She tried to rob me, and then she tried to kill me!' he said. And myself, having grown curious," Hoannes said, "I peered from the cover of the ditch and saw the peddler carefully feel of the decoration the stone had left on his head.

'That old woman certainly packed a mean wallop,' the Arab said with a groan."

After hearing Hoannes relate his experience, Armen's spirits lifted—he felt a strong stirring to do more than just sit and accept their miserable existence. Mother, on the other hand, forbade Hoannes to attempt such missions again.

"It would be preferable to eat grass," she said, "than to reduce the remaining number of our family."

"But, Mother," Hoannes insisted, "if we are to survive, we must fight to live!"

"Son," she replied, "Jesus himself refused to fight back. To the ruler Pilate He replied, 'If my kingdom were of this world, my followers would fight.' But it is not, and they did not."

"Mother, shall we not even fight to stay alive?" Armen asked.

Mother responded gently, "When Christ, after being betrayed by Judas, was arrested by the Roman soldiers, what did His servant Peter do?"

With much gusto, Armen replied, "Peter drew his sword and cut a fellow's ear off!"

"And what was Jesus response?" asked Mother. "On the very eve of being condemned to be crucified?"

Hoannes sighed and answered, "He commanded Peter to put the sword away."

"And then what?" Mother asked. Hoannes looked away and would not answer.

"Jesus healed the scoundrel's ear," remarked Armen.

After that, with the boys being forbidden to attempt missions—and because their love and respect for their now-frail mother constrained them—life at the camp moved about in a hopeless, weary circle, day after long, hungry day. But amidst this monotony, one evening a very strange and terrible thing happened. A feeble-looking old man, carrying a bundle and using a staff, went about the Nevsher remnant, inquiring for the Arakelians. When at last he found them, he introduced himself: he was a Turk by the name of Osmun Bey. "I was a good friend of your husband, Hagop," he told Agayne. "I am in trouble with my own people and am trying to escape, but I want to talk to you before I go on."

The story he relayed next brought great sobs from Mother. Meanwhile, being disguised as old women, Armen and Hoannes were forced to silently play the part of disinterested listeners. They were far from disinterested, but fiercely grieved, as they listened to the Turk claim to have seen their dear sister Parease die; he wanted her mother to know that her beautiful daughter had refused to deny her faith, even to death. Why a Turk felt compelled to hunt Mother up and tell her the sordid story, Armen did not know. Perhaps, knowing death was right at his heels, sympathy moved him. Shortly after telling Mother his story, the Turk was captured by his own people and shot to death.

Once again, the little family felt gripped by the depths of despair. Were it not for Mother leading the boys in great sobbing prayers, they would have found no peace. But, clinging together in prayer, they felt an unexplainable peace cover them. And so it was that the weary, hungry circle of days continued without further event. Until, that is, one night when they suddenly heard unusual activity outside their tent. The noise and commotion increased in volume as Armen, Agayne and Hoannes listened in the darkness. Their hearts beat in great throbs of fear. *What was to come to them next?*

Soon they were surrounded by chaos and shouting. "Get out of your tents, you lazy swine—pack up at once!" the soldiers bellowed. Armen's blood was suddenly charged with fear; it rippled through him in tiny bubbles.

"Hurry, hurry boys," Agayne whispered, "please don't let the soldiers come after us. We must be ready."

Outside the tent guards swarmed, bleating out orders. They used clubs and whips to make the people move faster. Soon the prisoners were on the march again. Armen learned they were to be deported by train. No one in his family had ever seen a train before; they wished their first experience were under better circumstances. The noise of its approach and the strange light which shot through the darkness, as what seemed to Armen to be a huge monster bearing down upon them, successfully cooled his youthful anticipation. When the train came to a screeching stop, the soldiers literally beat the crowd into cattle cars. Feeble old people, women with babies, small children—it made no difference. They were pushed, kicked and clubbed. No mercy was shown; head or feet first, in they went.

Traveling in foul-smelling cattle cars, unable to even sit down, Armen, Hoannes and their mother—along with the rest of the suffering mass—were rushed along with not the slightest idea of their destination. For two days and nights the horrible journey continued. Being packed so tightly was fatal for many people, including those next to Armen . . . but they remained standing—even in death.

Finally, the train came to a halt at a place called Gutmo, in Arabia. Within a few days of their arrival, an epidemic of malaria spread throughout the camp. Armen was among those who contracted the disease. Most of the victims succumbed to death, but Armen survived. Slowly he recovered from delirium and returned to reality.

After two months at Gutmo, the death march resumed. By this time, many Armenians had lost the will to live. Armen constantly heard cries of despair as people begged their captors, "Kill me and be done with it—for God's sake, kill me and put me out of my misery! I can't go on." Had it not been for Armen's mother and brother encouraging him to remain strong, he too would have given up.

There were times Hoannes literally carried Armen on his back because he was too weak to move any further.

The next stop was a place known as Ras-Ul-Ain, located close to the city of Baghdad. It was not completely in the desert, so the people were relieved to find a fresh water stream there.

Armen soon observed soldiers dressed in full military attire; some wore the traditional "red fez"—a felt hat with a black tassel attached to the top. Even the horses were well groomed. "What do you think is going to happen now?" Armen asked Hoannes.

"I don't know, Armen, but it looks like a big day for somebody," Hoannes responded.

Shortly afterward, a large man dressed in a Turkish uniform exited the train. He was the Minister of Interior, Talaat Pasha, who came to inspect the area. After his inspection, he announced to the guards:

"There are far too many Christians left!"

After the Minister departed, Armen, Agayne and Hoannes listened to the heartbreaking cries of babies—and their mothers—throughout the camp as guards ripped infants and toddlers from their mother's arms. The little children were tossed into carts like garbage. Mothers who tried, in desperation, to protect their children were killed instantly.

The guards filled the carts, then drug them away from camp. The little bodies of the children were dumped in a landfill about a half mile away, then they were set on fire.

Amidst the guttural sobs, moans and wails of those who had lost their beloved children, Agayne, Armen and Ho-annes wept and clung together. Agayne turned her eyes toward Heaven and reached for a way to pull Armen and Hoannes up toward hope. In low, firm tones, she began to speak:

"The Lord is my shepherd; I shall not want. He maketh me to lie down in green pastures; He leadeth me beside the still waters. He restoreth my soul: He leadeth me in the paths of righteousness for His name's sake. Yea, though I walk through the valley of the shadow of death, I will fear no evil: for Thou art with me: Thy rod and Thy staff they comfort me. Thou preparest a table before me in the presence of mine enemies: Thou anointest my head with oil: my cup runneth over. Surely goodness and mercy shall follow me all the days of my life and I shall dwell in the house of the Lord forever."

That night the moon turned blood red.

SIX

"Be thou faithful unto death, and I will give thee a crown of life." Revelation 2:10b

The first of the Bedawee warriors appeared over the highest sand dune just after noon. Earlier that morning, as the faintest rays of light crested the barren horizon, and the thick heat of the desert settled over the ragged prisoners, Armen had mourned the arrival of another day. When the order to march pulled him reluctantly to his feet, he'd also mourned the loss of his brother, whom they hadn't spotted in many days.

From Ras-Ul-Ain, the crowd of people had been driven on foot through the Syrian Desert. On the second day, as they plodded along, Mother had noticed an old friend up ahead stagger and stumble, trying to keep up with the others. Mother immediately sent Hoannes to the elderly woman's aid, much against his own wish. As Hoannes had predicted, Armen and Mother missed Hoannes' stalwart strength. They soon began to lag behind. Armen begged Mother to recall Hoannes, but remembering the weakness of her elderly friend, she refused. Due to this arrangement, within a few days Armen and Agayne had lost sight of Hoannes. The majority of the captives were driven along at a pace that Armen and Mother could not keep up with. When the distance between the two groups widened, Armen and Mother found themselves traveling among the small crowd of tail-enders that consisted of the elderly, the ill and crippled, or those with tiny children.

The morning drug along, and Armen's mood grew dark and bitter as he struggled to keep his mother on her feet— oh, how he missed his brother! The severe conditions of the desert weakened old and young alike. Armen lacked the strength of Hoannes, who had often held them both up.

Although Mother continued to take small steps beside him and gently squeeze his arm, he feared she was slipping away. Yet, for all the frailty Armen saw and felt in her body, Mother's spirit did not dim nor was she silenced.

Leaning upon his arm, she recited softly as they hobbled along, "For I know the thoughts that I think toward you, saith the Lord, thoughts of peace, and not of evil, to give you an expected end. Then shall ye call upon me, and ye shall go and pray unto me, and I will hearken unto you. And ye shall seek me, and find me, when ye shall search for me with all your heart."

Stopping to breathe deeply, she asked, "Will you promise to do this for me, Armen?"

"I will try, Mother," he answered.

"Seek Him with all of your heart. He will be with you, my beloved son, even if your mother cannot be."

"Please, Mother," he begged, "do not leave me!" Armen was terrified and choleric at the thought of losing her. *What would he do without his mother?*

Once again she leaned upon his arm and began taking halting steps forward. "Armen," she replied, "remember what I have taught you; Jesus saith, I am the resurrection, and the life: he that believeth in me, though he were dead, yet shall he live."

Mother instilled in him a love for the Holy scriptures from an early age. Armen had looked up to his father; Hagop was a man of faith and character, always hard-working and dependable. But Mother had a way of bringing the Bible to life. Throughout his childhood, Armen had been particularly interested in biblical events that occurred in Nevsher (called Cappadocia in scripture). In early Christianity, persecuted believers hid in his hometown as they fled Roman authorities. The apostle Paul also preached his first sermon in their region. However, despite his previous interest, Armen's understanding and concern for the things of God were no match for the despair and horror that now consumed their lives. For many dark days he had tried to *reason through* his confusion. At last he'd reached a conclusion. But before he voiced his thought, Mother responded.

"Son, God has not forsaken us! I can't tell you yet why our blessed Savior has allowed this. But I know, and trustingly believe, that it was permitted for some good purpose, which will be revealed in that day when we see our Lord Jesus face to face."

Armen made no reply. He could no longer see evidence of God's blessings nor of the Almighty's goodness—for if He truly were *almighty* and *good*, He would have stopped their suffering by now. Many times Mother said that the Turks could not help themselves, for the poor, lost souls did not know God. But it was much more difficult to be satisfied with such an answer now; the Turks may not have been able to stop themselves, but certainly an *almighty, good* God could have stopped them!

Armen glanced about at the struggling crowd around them and the ever-present mounted Turkish guards who flanked them on all sides. Mother had long told him that God loved even the Turks—even those whose beliefs and actions made them objects of His wrath. This too was incomprehensible. "Armen, while we were yet sinners, Christ died for us," she had said many times. "God's love is unconditional," she'd told him, "for *God is love*—He sends the blessing of rain upon the wicked and the good; He feeds and waters His enemies; He breathes the breath of life into them; He offers constant reminders of His love and patient days to repent and accept His path of salvation. God's love is unconditional, but salvation is not. Narrow is the gate and few there are that find it. Armen, many people are merely religious; they do not know Christ, therefore, they do not truly know the Father. Promise me that you will seek to know the difference," she had begged. "Promise me that you will find the narrow gate, and enter in."

Armen's spirit was bruised, and his outlook was warped by the suffering about him. Though his mother was as dear to him as life itself, he could not see things as she saw them. But still she continued to pour out her mother-love and words as they trudged along.

The morning grew longer and their steps shorter. Agayne put one foot in front of the other and clung to Armen now with what remained of her strength. In time they entered a section of desert where other prisoners ahead of them, despite their sufferings, had left a message for those who followed. In charcoal letters upon the rocks, they had written:

"As Jesus did not deny us, do not deny Him. We have not denied Him. Follow us."

When Armen glanced at Mother's face, she was smiling. As the day drug on, she continued smiling affectionately at Armen and speaking many more words—as many as her feeble body had the breath for. And Armen continued to hold tightly to his precious mother.

In the late morning, however, the weary crowd of tail-enders became restless as they entered a part of the desert known to have dangerous Bedawee tribes lurking nearby. They could no longer see the larger crowd of Armenian captives ahead of them; they and their guards had no doubt passed through this section of the desert already. Without the protection of the larger group and the many guards who drove them along, the small group of strag-glers, made up of only the weakest, were greatly afraid. Bedawees were known to pick off the slow and the weak, as well as those who traveled alone. There were many tribes of these wild, lawless people in the desert; they were nomadic in disposition and robbers and murderers by profession. It was believed these wild nomads descended from Abraham's son, Ishmael. As if the Turks weren't bad enough, the fact that Bedawees were nearby brought new terror to Armen. He was only glad that his brother Hoannes was traveling in the large group that had already crossed this section of the desert.

Just after noon, while the sun boiled high above and its heat danced across the hot desert sand, an extreme feeling of uneasiness began to grip Armen. At one point, he was almost sure he'd seen horsemen in the distance. As the long moments drug by, the hazy glimpses grew more frequent until, at last, he was certain he saw horsemen traveling toward the small crowd of Armenians. Once again he longed for the comforting presence of Hoannes and his greater strength, but he was undoubtedly miles ahead.

Suddenly—as if out of nowhere—the howling warriors appeared over the sand dunes, rushing on horse-back toward the crowd of Armenians. Their terrifying shrieks echoed off the dunes, and Armen felt as if his blood seemed to congeal; a heaviness seized his feet and legs. As the riders hurled ever nearer, their dark eyes and gloomy faces became visible. They were carrying ropes and scimitars; the sunlight shimmered and glinted on the short, curved blades of their weapons. The warrior's swift Arabian horses snorted and whinnied; their graceful feet thundered across the desert, sending sprays of sand out behind them where their proud tails flew high like flags.

"Hyroo-o-o-o! Hyroo-o-o-o!" the warriors bellowed.

The next thing Armen knew, the small crowd of tail-enders around him began falling beneath the weight of galloping horses and flashing blades. In the air above him, ropes swirled and flew. Hearing the sound of his heart hammering, he watched the noose of a coarse rope float through the air — as if in slow-motion — and settle beside him, over the head of his dear mother. In an instant, Mother was pulled off her feet and whisked from his side.

Armen raced after her, crying out.

When at last he reached her, it was too late. Mother was gone . . .

Neither pain, nor loss, but rage filled him. Hot adrenaline shot through his body; like *Samson* in the Bible, Armen burst to his feet and went after the nearest warriors. Intent upon revenge, he attacked them fiercely. Moments later, Armen found himself lying on the sand beside Mother. An open wound to his leg gushed his own blood into the searing sand beside her. Beneath the bright, hot orb of the sun, Armen was plunged into darkness.

How long he lay beside Mother's still body, he wasn't sure. By the time he blinked and looked around, his rage had cooled and his blood congealed. Gazing at his surroundings, he saw there were no more horses, no more warriors and no Armenians standing. The lifeless crowd was now strewn across a blood-stained desert.

Suddenly, Armen's thoughts were interrupted by the sound of weeping. Encouraged by the sound of life, mournful as it was, Armen slowly lifted his body from the sand and limped toward the cries. Cresting a low sand dune, he found the frail figure of an old, blind man. Between his weeping, the old man continually called out for his daughter. But there was no reply. Armen stood near the man, silent, unable to find words. After a time, the man began to pray, so Armen bowed his head.

"Oh God, giver of every good and perfect gift," the blind man cried out, "be merciful to me and send me help or death. In the Name of Christ, I ask. Amen." Shortly after praying, the old man drew in a long and labored breath, then let it out slowly. He did not draw another.

In time, Armen noticed that vultures had begun to circle above. With a heavy heart, he rushed back to his fallen mother, knelt in the sand beside her and began to dig with his hands. Despite his weakness, he continued to dig until he'd fashioned a deep bed in the desert sand. When she was laid within, he covered her fully.

Choking back tears, Armen recited one of Mother's favorite scriptures: the 23rd Psalm. He then softly sang the "Hyer Mer" *(The Lord's Prayer)*, a beloved song they used to sing every Sunday in church.

He stood trembling for many long moments afterward. Mother was gone. She had taught him that her body was only an earthly shell for a spirit whose devotion to Christ would wing her to Heaven. Even if God had abandoned the Armenian people, Armen felt certain that God would never abandon his faithful mother. She was the godliest person he'd ever known. Still, it was impossible to walk away . . . Armen's understanding and devotion were very weak. He doubted whether their faith was really worth dying for. But, if there was one thing he knew for sure, he knew that his mother would not want him to grieve like those who had no hope. And if his dear father were alive, he would tell him to pray for help and understanding. So, at last, Armen prayed for understanding and the strength to go on.

As the sun glared off the desert around him and the heat waves drifted over Mother's grave, he wiped at his tears with the sleeve of his now-ragged old costume, said one last goodbye, then turned and walked away. The Lord had answered his prayer.

> *Beautiful bride of Jesus, beautiful bride Agayne.*
> *Welcome to my kingdom, I am your King of Kings.*
> *Rejoice and sing with gladness, my sweet desert rose,*
> *Your fragrance fills my garden, your love like water flows.*
>
> *Through the golden streets of heaven, she bows before God's throne.*
> *Precious bride of Jesus, my beloved Agayne is home.*
> *Clothed in the light of His glory, holy child of God.*
> *She's singing with the angels, now and forever more.*
> *She's dancing with her daughter, heaven's music fills the air.*
> *Dancing with their Savior, her beloved Parease is there.*
> *- By Sharon Bigelow*

SEVEN

"The Lord is thy keeper: the Lord is thy shade upon thy right hand. The sun shall not smite thee by day, nor the moon by night." Psalm 121: 5-6

Armen was now alone, limping his way through the desert. While it was without a doubt the darkest day of his life—his own *Gethsemane*—as he trudged slowly along, a scripture came to him as if to hold his hand and push him forward. It played over and over in his mind while the afternoon wore on.

The Lord shall preserve you from all evil; He shall preserve your soul. The Lord shall preserve your going out and your coming in, from this time forth, and even forevermore . . .

He didn't entirely believe that the Lord would preserve him from all evil, but the scripture stuck within his mind nonetheless. The only remaining hope he had was that he might find Hoannes alive. So, with that small hope and the scripture encouraging him, he continued on.

After walking for a few hours, Armen approached a railroad station run by Turkish officers. This was the first sign of life he'd seen since the old, blind man died. As soon as they saw him, he was immediately handed over to the sergeant—a man by the name of Musa Ali.

"Another doddering old Christian dog, huh?" Musa asked. "Throw her in the stable! I'll dispose of her later!"

That evening Musa Ali visited the stable. Armen was confused when he heard the same man who mistreated him earlier now speaking in the Armenian tongue. "Look," Musa whispered in a compassionate voice, "look and be not afraid." Musa held out a golden cross.

Armen recognized the emblem—it represented the Armenian church. *Has God sent me an angel?* Armen wondered. However, he remained wary and silent.

When Musa was sure they wouldn't be overheard, he informed Armen that, when he joined the Turkish army, he had only pretended to be a convert to Islam. "In reality," Musa whispered, "I suppose I am a self-appointed spy, committed to helping my people survive."

At last convinced, Armen relaxed. "Thank you, Sir. May God bless you," Armen said.

Instantly the sergeant looked both startled and confused. "Your voice is not that of a woman," Musa said.

"I'm not an old woman, but only a boy trying to escape from the Turks," Armen answered.

"Your disguise and actions completely fooled me," Musa replied. "I am certainly glad you're a boy, for it will be much easier to help you!"

For seven days Armen remained in the stable resting and eating the nutritious food Musa provided. Although Musa wished to find a way to free him, Armen finally convinced his new friend to help him rejoin the larger crowd of Armenian prisoners that he had been separated from. Although Armen longed to be free, his desire to find his brother was too strong; in order to search for Hoannes, he was willing to become a captive again, knowing it would mean almost certain death. Reluctantly, Musa finally agreed; he arranged for an escort to accompany Armen within a mile of the camp where he believed Hoannes might be held. After that, without knowing what to expect, Armen was on his own.

Once inside the prison camp, hours went by before Armen finally spotted his brother, Hoannes. His older brother had grown far thinner and now looked very frail. But when he saw Armen, Hoannes eyes lit up. No words were necessary; Hoannes knew that their mother was gone.

Hurrying forward, the boys embraced, cried and clung to each other. Despite the overwhelming pain of losing Mother, Armen was greatly encouraged by the presence of Hoannes. He quickly noticed that the changes in his brother were not merely outward; although Hoannes was far weaker physically, he had gained an inner strength and tranquility. Hoannes reminded Armen more of Mother now than ever before. On the first night they were reunited, the boys slipped outside to gaze at the stars.

"I imagine Mother is at peace now," Armen said.

Closing his eyes, Hoannes replied, "Yes, Mother is at peace with her blessed Savior."

Bowing his head, Hoannes recited, "The Lord is my shepherd; I shall not want. He maketh me to lie down in green pastures; He leadeth me beside the still waters. He restoreth my soul: He leadeth me in the paths of righteousness for His name's sake.

"Yea, though I walk through the valley of the shadow of death, I will fear no evil: for Thou art with me: Thy rod and Thy staff they comfort me. Thou preparest a table before me in the presence of mine enemies: Thou anointest my head with oil: my cup runneth over. Surely goodness and mercy shall follow me all the days of my life and I shall dwell in the house of the Lord forever."

 eight

Summer, 1914
Syrian Desert

"Seek the Lord and his strength, seek his face continually."
1 Chronicles 16:11

Now that Armen was reunited with the crowd of Armenian captives, he once again was subject to the cruel routine of their Turkish captors. Despite their great feebleness and a strong wind, Armen and Hoannes rose early the next morning—upon command—and began the day's long trek, side by side. The winds fought against them as they went, blowing their gaunt frames about and stinging their faces with sand. Onward they staggered, regardless, urged forward by the guards. The small crowd around them also labored along silently, having not the vigor to talk.

Some time later, when the guards moved to the back of the crowd, the people began to speak amongst themselves. They suspected something was wrong.

Within moments, the loud, eerie cry of the Bedawees rent the air around them. *"Hyroo-o-o-o! Hyroo-o-o-o!"*

The crowd erupted in screams of terror as nearly a dozen large, half-clothed men with tattooed faces crested a small rise and rushed toward them. Atop their heads the warriors wore colorful turbans, decked with human bones. In their fists they gripped sharp swords. Raising their swords, they began swinging as they advanced through the cowering crowd.

Armen cried out, pressing closer to his beloved brother; he wept and shook uncontrollably as those they had traveled with fell around him. Drawing him nearer, Hoannes encircled Armen with his arms and held him tightly.

"It's alright. I will protect you," Hoannes whispered hoarsely.

Days passed before Armen awoke in a daze. The first thing he noticed was intense pain . . . his throat throbbed. Lifting a weak arm, Armen put his hand to his neck and felt coarse bandaging. As his eyes began to focus, he examined the dimly-lit space around him. He was lying on a thick bed of ferns, deep inside what looked like a cave.

A strange young woman was by his side. She held a small, flickering candle, and her face was covered with tattoo marks.

"Oh! You're awake!," she exclaimed, flashing a toothless smile. Her face lit with joy as she gazed down at him.

"Where am I?" Armen asked. His faint, rasping voice surprised even him. He tried to sit up, but he was too weak, and the pain in his neck became almost unbearable as he moved. He lay back, groaning.

"Don't worry. Try to rest," she answered. "You're safe here if you keep very quiet. Eat of the bread and water beside you. I cannot stay, but I will come back soon," she said.

"Who are you?" he asked.

"I am Zartar," she replied. "And I am joyful that my God has heard my cries and woken you!"

After that, Zartar vanished into the darkness, leaving food and water on the ground beside him. As soon as his strength allowed him, Armen ate some of the bread and drank some of the water. Afterward, in the silence and near-darkness, Armen lay still, wondering. Where exactly was he? Hoannes had indeed protected him, just as he'd promised. It appeared he'd also found them a hiding place. Now where was his brother? After so much suffering and bloodshed all around, why were they still alive? Holding his hand back up to his throat, Armen pondered these things. Surely it was the Lord's doing. The Lord had saved them again. But why?

After all of his lack of devotion and the wrong thoughts he'd been having, Armen knew he was thoroughly undeserving. He had noticed a change in Hoannes; his faith had grown stronger. Surely God was pleased with Hoannes. But that God would continue to spare Armen's life, when he had not earned God's favor, puzzled him. For perhaps the first time ever, Armen felt as if he were a sinner. Not only the wicked Turks, but he—a beloved Armenian son—was a sinner! He, who had thought he'd worshiped the Lord Jesus from birth, could suddenly see that his devotion to God was highly dependent upon circumstances. If God blessed his family; if God blessed the Armenian people—when God *made sense to him*—then Armen was a devoted Christian. But outside those parameters, his devotion to that same Jesus wavered. As Armen realized this, he suddenly had a fear of God that he had never experienced before. He had been faithless, yet God continued to save him?

That night, alone in the darkness, he thanked God for the gift of Christ. He thanked God that His own strong arm had made a way, through the death of His perfect and sinless Son, that Armen might be forgiven. With a deep sense of gratitude, Armen bowed his head and vowed to surrender his life to Christ.

In the morning, his spirit was refreshed from the warm rays of the sun shining in around him. He realized he was indeed inside a small cavern; it had a low roof and the ground was covered in ferns. He peered through the opening and was relieved to see he was in the middle of an oasis. He hoped that his brother was near.

Later that evening, the tattooed woman returned and patted him on the shoulder. "Dagha! Dagha! Wake up. I must change your bandage," she said. "Are you better?"

"I—I think so," Armen replied hoarsely.

"Try to sit up. I can manage better, I think." After propping him up, she applied a soothing lotion to his wound. "Two or three more dressings like this and the soreness will be almost out of your neck," she said.

"Will you tell me how I came here and why you are being so heavenly kind to me?" Armen asked.

"You are near the camp of the Bedawees who killed your people," she answered.

After he heard this, Armen began shaking as he remembered the massacres.

"Some other time I tell you," the young woman said.

"No, No! I want to know now," Armen cried out.

"Well, always after a killing, our Bedawee masters send us out to . . . to, well . . . strip the bodies of clothing and anything else of value," she said, looking down. "This is how I happened to find you clasped in the arms of a headless body."

In an instant, Armen knew that he'd only been fooling himself and trying to forget what he knew to be true. He hadn't truly expected that Hoannes could have brought him to this hiding place. "Oh, Hoannes!" he sobbed. "Oh, my brother!" Armen's sobs were deep and loud; immediately Zartar, gently, but firmly, placed a hand over his mouth.

"It is too dangerous!" she whispered. When Armen's sobs grew quiet, Zartar continued to speak softly. "I was startled to feel your heart beating. I wanted to save you, so I covered you the best I could. I left you until midnight, when our masters go marauding. Then I went back, found you and carried you to this cave. I dressed your wound and have been nursing you ever since."

"How long have I been here?" Armen whispered, in a voice thick with grief.

"You were unconscious three days, but you are doing finely now, and I am going to help you escape," she answered.

"But I have nowhere to go and no one left in the world," Armen responded.

"Any place is better than near this camp," Zartar said. "These creatures are worse than cannibals." Then she spoke in Armenian saying, "You must get away! I pray to my master Jesus that He'll show us a way."

Armen was puzzled. "You are a Christian? Yet you live in a camp of savage murderers?"

"I am a Christian, yes," Zartar answered. "But also I am a captive of these savages. My master extracted all of my visible teeth and covered my face with his horrible marks to crush my desire to escape. But he cannot crush my desire to help others escape! In all the years I have been captive, I have longed and prayed for a chance to help an Armenian. You are the first that was not killed outright, so I shall save you, no matter what suffering it may cost me!"

Together they bowed their heads and asked God to make a way possible for Armen's escape. Then, once again, Zartar disappeared into the night.

NINE

Several nights later, Zartar returned to the cave. She couldn't hide the excitement in her voice. "I have found a way for your escape!" she declared. "These Bedawees trade in camels and camel hides. This morning I heard the chief talking to the men about one of these trips to Mosul. In about a week they'll be leaving, and you will go with them!" Beneath her many tattoos (and despite her lack of teeth), Zartar's face beamed with the largest smile Armen had seen in a very long time.

"I'll leave with them?" Armen asked; the tone of his voice gave away his doubt and fear.

"Yes! The camel hides are packed in large bags and slung over the backs of the camels. They are loaded the night before—"

"But how will I go with them?" Armen interrupted.

"Well, now listen—I'll put you in one of those bags. It will be a hardship for a bit, of course, but it will mean freedom in the end," she replied. "You must do exactly as I tell you."

"Oh! I will—I promise you," Armen exclaimed. The hope of freedom suddenly burst forth in his heart and he found himself smiling widely as well.

After Zartar's announcement, Armen's days passed even more slowly. He had begun to move about the cave as much as possible, regaining his strength and preparing for his escape.

Now, although Armen agreed that Zartar's plan might work—and it was his only option—he needed to prepare mentally as well; he was in for another long, life-threatening journey.

When at last the day arrived, Armen begged Zartar to go with him.

"My dear boy, it makes me happy to know you think of poor Zartar, and I thank you," she replied. "But toothless me, with my marked face for all the world to read . . . " Zartar lifted her firm chin and shook her head slowly back and forth. "No, I never could get away. Now listen—"

Armen interrupted her, "What should it matter that your face is marked and you've missing teeth?"

"It matters," she replied. "Now listen, I am going to mark you, just one little bit, so when you are far away and have reached a happy life, you will remember Zartar and all others who are in trouble and help them if you can."

"Zartar," he begged, "you've said these warriors are little more than cannibals. Let me help you now! Come with me and escape!"

"You remind me of my very stubborn baby brother," she said with a weary sigh. "It is no wonder that of all those I have found, you have been the only one alive. God has special plans for you. But there is no escape for Zartar, dear boy. I will be satisfied to help you reach a happy life."

But Armen begged again, "Please come!"

Suddenly Zartar's strong chin trembled, and her eyes filled with tears; Armen was sure she would say yes. But just as suddenly as her expression had softened, it hardened again. "Sonny," she said, shaking her head, "You are a child, and a dear one. Others would not be so kind to one ruined like me. Now, when you're far away and live a happy life," she repeated, "look upon these noble marks that I give you, and remember Zartar and all others who are in misery. Will you promise this, Sonny?"

Armen nodded sadly. "Of course, Zartar," he said. "Although I won't *need* a mark to remember your wonderful kindness. How will you mark me?"

"Just a bit of a tattoo," she answered, opening the bag tied at her waist. "See, I do it this way." Using a sharp needle and bits of charcoal paste on Armen's forearm, Zartar inscribed his name, a sword, revolver and an Arabian gun.

Finally, the time came for his escape. Zartar helped him into a huge bag of foul-smelling camel hides. The bag closed by a zipper at the top; it was made with rope, instead of metal. She gave him supplies of food, water and a sharp, little knife. Before leaving, Zartar showed him how to open the bag for fresh air during the night.

When it was time to say good-bye, no words could express Armen's feelings. A combination of hope and despair gripped his soul.

"Live a good, clean life always, and remember me in your prayers; that is all I ask," Zartar whispered.

Armen's eyes filled with tears. Respectfully, he kissed her hand and bade her farewell. Ducking down inside the bag, Armen choked on the thick odor as he listened to Zartar's tender footfalls on the sand fade away to be replaced by the desert's night sounds.

Ten

*"He shall cover thee with his feathers, and under his wings
shalt thou trust: his truth shall be thy shield and buckler."*
Psalm 91:4

At sunset, the caravan began to move. Between the
foul odor and the rocky motions of the camel, Armen became nauseous. He wondered how he
was ever going to endure a three week journey. But he
thought about Zartar's bravery and how she risked her
life to help him escape. Her strength of character gave him
the determination to succeed.

Nearly three weeks later, as the caravan stopped to rest
near the city of Mosul, Armen peeked through the poke
holes and spotted a large raft near the river bank that was
being prepared for the marketplace. He knew at once that
this might be his only chance of escape.

"I must wait for the right time, when the Bedawees are
asleep, to make my escape," he whispered to no one but
himself—as had become his custom after spending so
long in the bag of camel hides.

When at last the prospect of freedom looked possible,
carefully, Armen cut the bag and slowly stepped outside;
his legs were weak and wobbly. Breathing in the fresh air
was rejuvenating. Summoning what little strength he had

left, he managed to stay on his feet and make his way quietly and safely to the raft. There he found a new hiding place, under a cargo of melons.

Finally, Armen reached the marketplace in Mosul. Still disguised as an old woman, he slipped away from the raft and into the crowd, without being noticed. He was free.

Now what?

Oblivious to everything around him, he wandered aimlessly around the city. He had nothing but the clothes on his back and the little knife Zartar had given him. By now his food rations were gone, but he was too exhausted to be hungry. Filthy from the long days and nights in the camel bag, Armen trudged across town. He was desperately alone.

How much time passed, he could not tell. It mattered not if he went in circles; he had neither deadline, nor destination. If only Mother would return to him; the cruelest of days at her side were better than this freedom. Many times Armen stumbled and fell; jarred by those passing by, his weak legs tangled in his now-torn, old skirts and he landed face-down.

How he longed to cry out, "Hoannes! I've fallen and need your help!" But, of course, no help would come. Armen had not Mother, Father, sister, nor the many older brothers who had so often borne him upon their shoulders as a younger child. Sometimes Armen lie silent for quite awhile before he had the strength to rise on his own.

Again and again his mind clouded, and he became confused. Eventually, Armen's thoughts grew dark. He pondered whether death might be preferable to his existence.
What good was life without those whom he loved? Without any who loved him? This sort of life was not life at all.
Yes, he finally decided, death would be preferable. He
wanted to die. He began to ponder death and to wonder
how he might find it.

But suddenly, as if the voice of God were answering,
church bells rang out loudly from a distance, more loudly
than seemed likely. They beckoned to him. *Come*, they
seemed to call. *Come, come quickly! Come and find shelter in
a house of worship!* Turning toward the familiar, old sound,
Armen stumbled along through the streets until he
reached the source of the mesmerizing tones. Climbing
the church steps, he stumbled into the stone building, entered the sanctuary and promptly collapsed, unconscious.

Much later, when he opened his eyes, Armen was surprised to find himself in a bed—the first real bed he had
seen in a long time. Gazing about, he saw two of the kind-
est-looking people he'd ever seen. They were speaking in
soft, comforting tones. He couldn't quite make out what
they were saying, but he understood the warmth in their
smiles. Like Musa Ali and Zartar, this couple were sent
from Heaven to look after him.

God had intervened, again, sparing Armen from death.

eleven

Anneza
October, 1914

"He shall not be afraid of evil tidings: his heart is fixed, trusting in the Lord." Psalm 112:7

Holding little Serapi in her arms, Anneza tiptoed away from the front room as the loud knocking sounded upon the front door again. With pounding heart, she rushed down the small hallway toward the back of their cottage. She hoped Serapi wouldn't awake and alert the person on the doorstep of their presence. No doubt it was their neighbor Defjian again. Earlier that morning she'd glimpsed him through shuttered blinds, pounding upon their door shortly after Mother left. She had not opened the door then, and eventually he'd gone away. However, now it seemed that he'd returned. Anneza couldn't imagine why the young man would persist in calling when Mother was gone, and she was certain she never wanted to find out.

Knock! Knock! Knock!

Her little sister Serapi jumped and fussed in her sleep as the banging came again, but just then Anneza reached the farthest back room, ducked inside and quietly closed the large, wooden door behind her. Serapi wouldn't hear the noise from here nor would their knocking-neighbor hear the fussing of the baby.

As much as Anneza tried not to complain, she found herself doing so lately. Though she dearly loved caring for her baby sister, she intensely disliked being left home alone. Mother now did all of her errands without Anneza's help, including gathering roka. On her own Mother took much longer. Anneza's brothers were away nearly all of the time as well; they attended the Mission school when not tending the barber shop. At the beginning of the school year the missionaries opened the girl's orphanage school in Hadjin and the boy's school in Everek. They were hopeful, they said, although the unrest in the country was becoming more violent and threatening each day. Because the Gregorian girls school in Hadjin didn't open, due to lack of funding from Constantinople, attendance at the missionary school soared. Nevertheless, as the first month of school finished up, despite the fact that her brothers were attending, Anneza was stuck at home—all day, every day—with her baby sister.

Of course she knew the evil actions of the Turks were to blame, but, to some degree, Anneza also blamed her neighbors for her confinement. Mrs. Hampartzoumian was a widow who had lived three houses down the street for as long as Anneza could remember. The soft-spoken old woman had just one surviving son, a young man named Kevork, or Defjian, who had immigrated to America in 1912 to meet up with a cousin in New York, leaving his mother alone. Hundreds of Armenian families from their region had now left their homes to immigrate to a land where they might have more liberty and safety. But widows, like Mrs. Hampartzoumian, lacked the means to leave. So when Mrs. Hampartzoumian received word that her son Kevork would be returning from America, she was overjoyed. Anneza, on the other hand, was not at all pleased. Anneza remembered Kevork very well.

Kevork, usually called Defjian, was a loner and a very melancholy young man. Not that Anneza blamed him. Just seven years before Anneza was born, Everek was plundered and burned during the massacre of November 18, 1895 — while Abdul Hamid was the Sultan of Turkey. Though just a young boy, Defjian had witnessed the ghastly murders of his brother and uncle. At the same time, the young women were taken captive by the Turks and assimilated into harems. The remaining Armenians were slaughtered, including babies.

Those who did survive escaped by hiding in caves. Among them were Mrs. Hampartzoumian, Defjian — who was quite young at the time — and even Anneza's mother, Vartuhi. They considered their survival a miracle. Anneza agreed. However, she didn't believe her neighbor Defjian had survived without lasting damage. The carnage he saw as a young boy had greatly affected him. No, Anneza was not happy that he had returned and would once again live next door.

On the day of his return, Vartuhi had invited the Hampartzoumians for a visit. It was supposed to be a joyful visit, but the conversation soon shifted as the women spoke of their many friends and relatives who had moved away. "My own sister and her family are packing," Anneza's mother Vartuhi said. "She begs me to follow. But with my five children to support—and no means to do that without the help of kind strangers—I can see no way . . ."

Mrs. Hampartzoumian nodded in agreement. "And with the missionaries leaving as well, surviving without a husband will grow harder still," the woman remarked. "You do know they've all been ordered home?"

Vartuhi nodded; apparently she'd known. To Anneza the news came as a shock. The missionaries were all leaving her country? What would become of the orphan boys? Wasn't this exactly what she'd feared would happen!? But, much to Anneza's distress, the conversation turned even worse, shifting next to the news of the hundreds of young women and girls recently abducted from nearby villages.

"Mrs. Ohanian, Anneza's becoming too pretty for her own good," Mrs. Hampartzoumian had warned. "I fear greatly for her safety, or lack of safety, should she be noticed!"

"Oh yes," her son Defjian had added, directing his comments directly at Anneza, "sweet Anneza is far too attractive. She will not escape notice."

Defjian had always made Anneza nervous; now that he'd returned from America, he downright frightened her. She

wished her mother had not invited Mrs. Hampartzoumian to visit.

"In times I have almost envied the evil Turks," Defjian
said. "Vile though they are, the Turks are not stupid—
they see our blossoming young women, prime examples
of womanhood, like sweet Anneza here, and they want
them. Why would they not? They have the approval of
their lecherous leaders to enjoy as many as they desire."
At Defjian's bold comment the older women began to
blush. Anneza felt heat rush into her face, as well, and
dropped her gaze to the rug upon the floor. She wished
she might hide. She also wished that it were time for the
Hampartzoumians to leave.

But instead, Defjian continued his rude commentary. "The
Turks need a constant replenishment for their lustful ap-
petites and diversions. Divorce is a very easy matter for a
Turk. In a moment of anger, he needs but say to his current wife, 'Cover thy face, thy *nekyah* is in thy hands,' and
she is no longer his wife. She must at once leave his home,
taking her belongings with her," he said.

"This low standard of family life is smiled upon by the
Sultan. His harem house, near Constantinople, is a castle,
not a house. Many girls are elected yearly to enter the Sultan's harem. The system is rotary, so while many are dismissed, the same number are elected. The servants are all
females, and no visitors are allowed. Pity; I'd have loved
to see inside." At this Defjian winked at Anneza and continued.

"The royal ship is anchored near the city, subject to the Sultan's slightest whim. When the whistle blows on the royal ship, all Constantinople knows that the Sultan is about to pay a visit to the harem house. And," Defjian added, "we need only use our imaginations to know what activities a visit includes."

At this, Mrs. Hampartzoumian cleared her throat and motioned to her son, shaking her head toward Anneza. With a glance in her direction, he replied, "Mother, Anneza, being old enough to arouse carnal interest, is fully old enough to engage in discourse on the matter."

At this declaration, Vartuhi's blush receded, replaced by a look of indignation. "There will be no such talk before my daughter," she said.

"Woman, you cannot escape the inevitable," Defjian replied smugly. "The harvest is fully underway; unless you intend to rid the world of the foul-minded Turk, the lush, ripe fruit you're growing here will soon be devoured. Furthermore—"

Interrupting, Mrs. Hampartzoumian rose from her feet and cried out, "Oh, my dear Mrs. Ohanian, I do beg your forgiveness!" Wringing her hands, the woman hurried toward the front door, motioning to her son to follow. "I am quite sure we have outstayed our welcome!" she said. "We will be going now!" With that declaration, the small woman all but drug her grown son from their home.

After the disturbing conversation with their neighbors, Vartuhi forbade her daughter to step foot outside. Anneza was a prisoner in her home because she'd been cursed with good looks—and the Hampartzoumians as neighbors.

However, her days were not all gloom. When there were no frightening persons poking about the cottage and banging upon the door, Anneza's favorite pastime was to sit at the front window and watch from behind the blinds as the orphan boys passed back and forth on the street. They carried loads of firewood that they would cut and store.

Anneza knew, all too well, why they did their work with such vigor and even joy; if they didn't gather enough firewood for the winter, they would have to use a fuel made from the refuse gathered from the streets after the herds passed by. She and her family would no doubt be using such fuel this winter . . . She was at least thankful that this time she would not be allowed to go out and gather it!

Just then, Anneza was jogged from her memories by the sound of the front door opening. "Anneza!?" her mother called out.

Quickly, Anneza carried her still-slumbering baby sister back toward the front room. Apparently her mother had returned early from gathering roka. Good! Mother's return should send the neighbor back down the street.

But as she entered the room, Anneza was very surprised, and nearly horrified, to see that just behind her mother stood her aunt, Mrs. Charvusian—on the doorstep.

"Anneza," her mother scolded, "you've left my poor sister standing in the cold. What were you thinking? Did you not hear her knocking at the door?!"

Anneza sighed and hung her head. What was she thinking, indeed! The next time there was a knock at the door she would risk peering through the blinds to see who it was.

Twelve

Armen

"Who led thee through that great and terrible wilderness, wherein were fiery serpents, and scorpions, and drought, where there was no water; who brought thee forth water out of the rock of flint." Deuteronomy 8:15

After inconceivable horrors, followed by days and nights stumbling aimlessly through the city of Mosul, the compassion he received within the home of the good couple who saved him seemed unreal. Once again, God had intervened, sparing Armen from death. But he did not feel *wholly alive.*

Nonetheless, under his host's loving care, his wounds gradually turned to scars and the heaviness of trauma faded, somewhat. When at last Armen recovered, the kind couple who nursed him—the Soulehmens—sent him to stay with a relative of theirs; his name was also Mr. Soulehmen, and he lived near a bathing resort community called Hammam Ali.

It was a quaint town with neighborhoods made of thatched huts and cottages. The community of Hammam Ali supplied a natural hot-spring, which was piped into a large pool. The fresh, flowing water reminded Armen of the pool of Bethesda mentioned in the Gospel of John. Like the ancients, many of the town's people believed this spring possessed healing properties.

Mr. Soulehmen owned a large herd of camels, which his family used to do business. The water for the pool at Hammam Ali was filtered from the ground through great tiers; they contained a large quantity of tar. On a regular basis, these tiers were discarded and delivered to Baghdad, using Mr. Soulehmen's camels as a means of transportation.

Before long, Armen began working for Mr. Soulehmen under the supervision of Obdul Omar, who trained him for a caravan job; it demanded many long weeks of travel. Armen's work with the caravan also involved the shipment of various fruits, such as figs, dates, pomegranates, melons and a mixed variety of nuts.

His favorite part of the job was working with the camels. Feeding time entertained him greatly. Each camel came forward to receive their share, after the drivers prepared the food by mixing dark, coarse chaff, flour, water and oil. As if they were playing a sport, the camel-drivers rolled the mixture into a ball and thrust it as far back into the camel's mouth as they could—sometimes using the full length of their arm! Armen watched in amazement; the creatures seemed to know the exact number they would receive.

Armen's meals practically consisted of the same ingredients the animals received, such as fine meals cooked in water and olive oil. Everyone ate from the same dish, using their fingers, while a large clay jug of water was passed around.

The Boss, a two-humped Bactrian camel, was the undisputed leader of the herd. The rest were Arabian camels, with only one hump. Armen's supervisor, Obdul, always rode beside the Boss on a donkey. Then, when it was time to rest, Obdul simply tapped the knees of the Boss camel, and he sat down. Immediately, the rest of the herd did likewise.

One day, Armen's caravan was transporting valuable wares across the desert. About sixty armed escorts on camels accompanied them, watching vigilantly for any signs of danger. They traveled without incident for many long miles, until suddenly, the guide (who held a huge telescope) signaled to the other escorts. In an instant, the escorts burst out ahead of the caravan, riding fast, until they were mere shapes on the distant horizon. Their advance signaled trouble for Obdul's caravan; immediately Obdul gave the sign, and the rest of the caravan slightly deviated from their course. In the desert ahead, the escorts confronted armed bandits, and a skirmish ensued. Remarkably, the escorts' camels were so well-trained that they automatically deposited their riders and ran for safety after the first shots were fired, leaving the men to fight on foot. When it was over, the camels obediently came out of hiding and returned to their travels.

After the excitement, the trip toward Baghdad continued in monotonous peace and safety. The next evening they stopped to rest, and Armen and the other drivers became curious when they spotted a large social gathering of Bedouins in the distance. They decided to camp nearby and soon learned that a wedding was about to be performed. The bride and groom were both the royal children of Sheiks. Before the ceremony could begin, the two leaders negotiated an acceptable bridal dowry (two horses, three camels, or so many lira). After the Sheiks reached an agreement, the wedding arrangements were immediately underway.

Armen and his co-workers were welcomed as guests; these Bedouin people were (surprisingly) as hospitable as they were warlike. Armen watched in wonder as, first, the servants crushed the coffee in a brass bowl using mallets and striking them to create a rhythmical beat. Then a *Mollah* (leader of the Mosque) conducted the ceremony. The bride, covered by a thick veil, was never seen.

A wonderful meal followed the ceremony; Armen was offered rice pilaf, lamb, fowls, soups and kibby—made of cracked wheat and meat pounded together, then placed on a tray layered with sliced onions, pine seeds and spice and baked in an oven. Lively music with tambourines and violins filled the desert air. The men and women were separated (as they would remain during all of the festivities), and Armen joined the other male guests as they formed groups and chanted while alternating back and forth in song.

That evening, while the music and chanting could still be heard, Armen found a place to sleep near the camels, laying his head on a sand pillow. Although the Bedouin's festivities would last for days, Armen's caravan would continue toward Baghdad with the rising of the sun; he needed rest and strength for the journey. Turning the mantle of his turban down to protect him from the chilly wind, Armen closed his eyes and drifted off to sleep; that night he dreamed of his mother, father and siblings. In his dreams they were alive and happy.

Thirteen

Anneza

"When thou passest through the waters, I will be with thee; and through the rivers, they shall not overflow thee: when thou walkest through the fire, thou shalt not be burned; neither shall the flame kindle upon thee. For I am the Lord thy God, the Holy One of Israel, thy Saviour . . ." Isaiah 43:2-3a

With each passing week, things changed more rapidly than ever. Not only had Anneza lost her freedom to come and go as before, all of her close childhood friends had now moved away. The only good Anneza saw in these developments was the fact that she had also outgrown all of her dresses and was ashamed to be seen. She alternated between stuffing herself into things that were too short and would not button, or floating and tripping around in one of her mother's much-too-large dresses—as she was doing this afternoon. The Charvusians—Anneza's aunt and uncle—had come again for a visit, which wasn't unusual. But unlike their many other visits, this would be the very last before they left for America.

Vartuhi had always been joyful when her sister came to visit. They laughed over fun memories and spoke fondly of beloved friends and relatives. They shared food and supplies. But lately, Anneza's mother didn't seem cheered by visits with her sister. They no longer had much to share nor could they speak of friends and family without weeping. Now their talk always reverted to the war. This day turned out to be the same, despite being the last time the sisters would be together. While Anneza's brothers were out visiting with their uncle and cousins, Anneza stood in the kitchen with the women, helping to prepare a meal from the small amount of meat her mother received from the missionaries and a few rare vegetables her aunt brought to share. She also kept a keen eye on little Serapi, who was playing with wooden spoons nearby. As usual, Anneza's aunt brought the family up-to-date with the latest events while they worked. "By now, practically the whole world is involved in this war! And I wish I had better news," she said in a disturbed voice, "but the Turks have closed the Dardanelle's Strait so Russia can no longer send support to the Allies or receive ammunition in return!"

"God help us," Vartuhi said, with a weary shake of her head. "They can't lose this war . . ."

"The Germans are behind it," her sister explained. "They sold two of their warships to the Ottomans — the Goeben and Bresla. But no one really believes the Ottomans own those vessels; they're still being run by German crewmen!"

Vartuhi sighed and waved her hand toward her sister. "Shhh," she said, "no more bad news. Just let me enjoy your presence."

In hushed tones, her sister continued, "The administration has officially declared *jihad*—Holy War—to rid the world of *infidels*."

"*Shhh*, quiet!" Vartuhi repeated. "The children will hear." It was true, even when Anneza's Aunt whispered, Anneza heard every word. She attempted to appear busy and unaffected, but when they spoke of war, Anneza's worries—and her longing for her father—made her stomach and heart ache.

Nevertheless, Anneza's aunt continued whispering, "Talaat's boasting that he's done more in three months to wipe out Christians in the Ottoman Empire than Abdul Hamid achieved in thirty years. The Turks boldly proclaim, 'Allah is our aid, and the prophet (Mohammed) is our support.'"

At this Vartuhi only shook her head sadly as her sister continued.

"Rumors say our Armenian soldiers, after being forced into the Turkish army, were all marched into the desert and executed," she said. At this Vartuhi shot her sister a look that finally silenced her. But in the quiet, her aunt's whispered words echoed in Anneza's mind. Not wanting the women to be alarmed by the tears flooding her eyes, Anneza reached forth and chose an onion to dice for the dish they were preparing. Neither woman actually said it, but Anneza understood by their tones. They both believed her father was dead.

"Vartuhi, you and the children should leave before things get worse," her sister warned, more loudly now. Vartuhi simply shook her head and sighed. Anneza silently agreed; with five children and no husband, her mother's only choice was to stay.

"You know," Vartuhi said at last, "it was an Armenian soldier who saved Enver Pasha from being taken prisoner-of-war by the Russians. Don't you remember? Enver Pasha sent a letter thanking our Archbishop for the heroism of our brave and noble men." The comment hung in the air between the two sisters. Yes, it was a fact. But who trusted the Ottomans to be fair and honorable, even to men they owed their lives to? Even Anneza's brother Garabed had told her that it was only natural the Turks would blame the Armenians for their loss after the terrible defeat at the Battle of Srikamish.

Much later, after dinner, the family gathered outside to relax on the flat roof of their home, enjoying the cool night air. Anneza carried her baby sister out into the refreshing air and deposited her on a soft carpet inside the playpen her mother had fashioned. As the days passed, little Serapi had learned to crawl, to pull herself up to stand and to babble. Her soft, dark hair had begun to form small curls about her ears and above her large, bright eyes. She also took far fewer naps during the day, which meant she was ready to sleep for the night at an earlier hour. Even now Serapi appeared very sleepy while she rested upon her rug watching her family visit. Anneza picked up her lyre and began to play softly for her sister while her mother spoke of war with her aunt and uncle, and her brothers played games with their cousins—war games, of course. It didn't seem good for a baby, nor for herself, to listen to so much dreadful talk; Anneza hoped the soothing music would drown most of it out. On her carpet nearby, Serapi smiled at the music; soon she began to nod her head and close her eyes. In this spot, surrounded by her family, Anneza could almost forget the troubles of her life. This had always been her favorite place, and she often went here to play the lyre her father had given her when she was quite young. She had always enjoyed the instrument. But now it was a priceless treasure.

At last, Vartuhi glanced up; with a look at Anneza, she motioned to the sleeping baby. Anneza set her lyre down, rose, took little Serapi gently into her arms and carried her down into their home. She hoped that Serapi hadn't heard the war-talk; it wouldn't be good for her to fall asleep with those words in her mind. Despite the fact that they were sisters, not mother and daughter, Anneza felt fiercely protective of her little sister.

"I'm here, Sera. I won't let anything harm you," Anneza told her often. Regardless of her own fearful state, Anneza spoke only bold and positive words for Serapi.

Now, as she placed her slowly into her crib, she whispered words of comfort—to the best of her ability. "The matter will turn out right, Serapi," she said. "God is aware of our troubles. He will protect you; you'll grow up to be a good and beautiful woman. And then, some day, you'll marry a good man." With those words, she kissed her and whispered, "Sleep well, Serapi, tomorrow is another day."

When Anneza returned to the roof, her family was still discussing the war. But the conversation seemed more hopeful as they spoke of the United States ambassador, Henry Morgenthau. Mr. and Mrs. Charvusian said the ambassador was doing everything within his power to stop the brutality of the Young Turks; nonetheless, he was unable to prevent it. Still, Anneza's relatives felt indebted to Morgenthau and respected his relentless labor on behalf of the Armenian people.

At last, when the light in the sky was gone, her brothers and cousins descended to the street below, and Anneza followed her family down the narrow stairway and inside their stone cottage. It was time to say their final goodbye to her aunt and uncle. But before a word was uttered, suddenly and violently, the ground shook under her feet, although she was no longer on the stairway. The air around her was rent by a deafening noise, as if the walls had exploded. When the ringing in Anneza's ears began to subside, she heard shrieking and the rapid footfalls of a crowd running through the streets outside their home. As her mother rushed to peer through the blinds, the front door burst open, and her older brother Garabed rushed inside, panting and wide-eyed.

"The Hampartzoumian's house has been bombed!" Garabed shouted.

fourteen

Armen

"The Lord is my rock, and my fortress, and my deliverer; my God, my strength, in whom I will trust; my buckler, and the horn of my salvation, and my high tower." Psalms 18:2

At the end of the season at Hammam Ali, Armen returned to the home of the kind couple, Mr. and Mrs. Soulehmen, who lived just outside the city of Mosul. They welcomed him gladly and treated him as a member of the family. Having time off from his travels and work was a welcomed break, and it also gave Armen the opportunity to catch up with the news; in the desert there had been very little information about the war. However, back in civilization, it was the main topic of conversation.

Daily Armen heard of the fierce fighting going on in many regions, including the Ararat Mountains. The Armenians had always believed that Mount Ararat was their rightful heritage; it was their pride—the center, one might say, of Armenia. Likewise the town of Van (located near the lake bearing the same name) was unusual in that its Armenian population exceeded the Moslem. Armenians considered Van one of their most important cities—but, of course, their claim to the region was disputed. Rumors that reached the Soulehmen household said that the towns in the Ararat section—Van and Bitlis—were war-torn and suffering.

When friends of the Soulehmens brought news from Van, Armen listened reluctantly, reliving the horrific memories of Nevsher. They reported that shortly after the war started, Djevdet Bey, a brother-in-law of Enver Pasha, was made Governor of Van. Djevdet Bey made demands on the Armenians of the territory which were impossible for them to fill at short notice. The situation grew more acute, until one evening two Armenian women, about to enter the city, were attacked by a group of Turkish soldiers. Several Armenian men went to the rescue and were shot dead. This immediately led to real shooting, and the battle was on. Many buildings were destroyed by bombardment, including several hospitals. The fighting spread to the nearby towns, until all the section around Van was drawn into it. Armenian men, women and children were massacred; homes, churches and schools were burned. In the nearby town of Bitlis, most of the Armenians were murdered. Nine hundred women and children were carried off and drowned in the Tigris River. At Diarbekr, not far from Bitlis, over seven hundred Armenian men, women and children were brutally executed, then dumped on a raft on the Tigris. Those coming from the region reported that the river was full of bodies and parts of bodies.

But eventually, the tales of horror and suffering were replaced by news that filled Armen with hope. There was great rejoicing in the Soulehmen household when they learned that the British had taken Basra, a city on the Tigris, not so far from Baghdad. Then one day, real excitement came. On that day, as Mr. Soulehmen arrived home, he rushed inside the house looking for Armen. "Armen, Armen!" he shouted in joy, "The British have taken the city of Mosul!"

Armen was equally excited by the news that the British had arrived and taken control of the city nearest him. He was certain this victory would change the entire course of his future.

Immediately upon gaining possession of Mosul, the British commander sent out a call for all Armenian refugees. Mr. Soulehmen hurried Armen to Mosul, where they found about seventy other Armenian boys gathered in the marketplace. With the aid of an interpreter, a British officer addressed them:

"You boys gathered here need help. The Turks have taken everything from you but your lives!" The officer paused and let his words hang in the air. The reminder stung; around him Armen saw other boy's faces reflecting the same aching pain that welled up inside him. At last, with a nod to acknowledge their great and terrible loss, the officer continued, "Boys, we purpose to do here just the same thing we have done in other places—namely, establish an Armenian Boy Scout Troop. There is a camp being prepared for this work just outside the city. In this camp you will live, learn and develop among your own kind of people, perhaps meeting again some of your own family. This camp will be ready in three days. Please report at that time. That will be all for today."

Armen walked away dazed. With neither Father, Mother, nor older siblings to consult, he did not know what to think. The officer's words stirred him; might he really be reunited with some of his relatives? He found it hard to consider parting with the kind Soulehmens, after all they had done for him. But although they treated him like family, he knew he was not.

Armen spent the next couple of days deep in thought. In the end, the British officer's words would not leave his mind; the Turks had taken his family from him! They had taken his home, his friends, his future; they had taken everything from Armen but his life! Now he was being offered a chance to do something about it. The more Armen pondered it, the stronger his hatred grew and the more he longed for revenge against the Turks, the murderers of his beloved family. The allurement of revenge and the chance to become part of a well-ordered military camp—whose enemy was also his enemy—was more than Armen could resist.

The next day, just before his fourteenth birthday, Armen entered the ranks and started life as a soldier boy. Replacements were needed in the region of Van. Armen and the rest of the newly formed troop of young Armenian boys were intended to be those replacements.

fifteen

Anneza

"For he shall give his angels charge over thee, to keep thee in all thy ways." Psalm 91:11

After the explosion of the Hampartzoumian's home, Anneza's uncle rushed out into the street, with the boys, to investigate. They found Mrs. Hampartzoumian, bruised but whole, standing before the remains of her home, screaming frantically. "My son! My son! Defjian—he's still inside!" she wailed.

Being a parent himself, Mr. Charvusian understood the woman's distress. Therefore, against his better judgment, he hastened into the smoking rubble, seeking the neighbor's son. Moments later, Mr. Charvusian emerged from the ruin that had been the Hampartzoumian's home; in his arms he carried Defjian, severely wounded and unconscious.

Meanwhile, Anneza sat silently with her mother and aunt inside the safety of their cottage, waiting for word and listening to the sounds of an agitated crowd in the street. After a very long time, the door opened and Anneza's brothers and cousins entered. Their expressions were extremely grim.

"Mother," Garabed said, "the Kaymakam has taken uncle away." The Kaymakam was the governor of their district; the Armenians in the region greatly feared this man.

"Everek's Kaymakam, Adil Bey, is questioning the witnesses, *Mam*," one of her cousins said to his mother, "and he accused Papa of being a witness!"

Mrs. Charvusian shook her head in confusion. "But what do they imagine your Papa has witnessed? He was here with us when the neighbors were attacked," she replied.

"Oh, but they were not attacked," Garabed answered. "Mrs. Hampartzoumian says Defjian was tinkering with a homemade bomb; he unintentionally blew himself up."

For the next six days, Mrs. Charvusian and her children shared beds and floor-space with the Ohanians. On the seventh day, Mr. Charvusian was finally released but commanded not to leave the region. This order mattered very little, at this point, for the Charvusian's ship had sailed without them. It would be quite some time before they could again secure passage on a ship to America. Reluctantly, the Charvusians returned to their own cottage to unpack, and the Ohanians attempted to return to some semblance of normality.

But normality was difficult to maintain while the world was embroiled in war; fears and suspicions were dangerously high across the district. Throughout Everek, reports quickly spread that Defjian's dread of imminent new massacres had agitated him enough to try to equip himself with the means of defensive resistance. Severely wounded and in excruciating pain, Defjian eventually died of his injuries. The Armenians of Everek were both frightened and surprised by the incident.

There wasn't a home or street in Everek where Defjian and his bomb incident wasn't the constant topic of conversation—including the Ohanian home. However, aware of the enormous danger hovering over the Armenian community as a whole, Everek's leaders chose to hush it up. Even Adil Bey, the Kaymakam on duty in Everek, agreed that it would be best to keep the Hampartzoumian bomb incident a secret. Given the law-abiding reputation and record of the town's Armenian population, Adil Bey concluded that a reckless individual, with no organizational ties or support whatsoever, had indulged in a dangerous adventure.

Yet not everyone in Everek agreed. A handyman at the local bakery, the only Turk in the neighborhood, thought it was wrong to conceal the matter. Therefore, he decided to contact higher authorities and inform them of the explosion. On the eighth day after Defjian's bomb incident, the secret of Everek was blown wide open; the Ohanian's hope of returning to normalcy evaporated forever.

Adil Bey was immediately dismissed. He was replaced by Salihzeki, who was his deputy and also the Kaymakam of the neighboring smaller town of Incesu. Salihzeki promptly launched a fierce and sweeping investigation, starting with the arrest of Defjian's family members, relatives and even casual acquaintances; he continued with the arrest of Armenians who had returned from America for short visits. At the first mention of the dismissal of Adil Bey, Anneza's mother, fearing arrest herself for having been a friend of Mrs. Hampartzoumian, gathered a small amount of belongings and fled Everek, taking her children to the caves to hide.

Meanwhile, the Kaymakam Salihzeki extended his arrests to include hundreds of other Armenians in neighboring villages and towns, the district's capital city and even in other major cities of the empire—including its capital, Constantinople. Overnight the district entered a time of intense torture that made the massacres of 1895 and 1909 pale in comparison. Everek's prison was transformed into (what would later be referred to as) *Dante's Inferno*. Within a short time, the other prisons of the district, such as Incesu, Comakhlu and especially the dungeon of Cafer Bey police station in the district's capital, Kayseri city, followed suit. The mass arrest, torture and execution of hundreds of its Armenian inhabitants, and the murderous deportation of the rest of the district's Armenian population, formed part of these measures.

In the surrounding districts, a number of churches were burned to the ground. Likewise, the orphanages in both Everek and Hadjin were shut down, and their buildings were burned. The surviving Armenians of the district scattered, as the Ohanians had, hiding wherever they could.

It was during this time of hiding that little Serapi learned to be very, very quiet—and to run. Meanwhile, Anneza's brothers grew to be young men, and Anneza matured into an exceptionally beautiful young woman who still spoke only words of comfort and hope to her beloved baby sister.

Late each night, while Serapi and the rest of her family slept, Anneza wept in fear and prayed to the Lord Jesus for deliverance.

sixteen

Armen

"And thine ears shall hear a word behind thee, saying, This is the way, walk ye in it, when ye turn to the right hand, and when ye turn to the left." Isaiah 30:21

In 1917, the United States of America also entered the Great War. In less than a year American involvement proved favorable for the Allied Powers. A major turning point ensued when the British set up naval blockades on German ports. As a result, thousands of Germans were starving. Many protested and held demonstrations throughout the streets of Berlin. These events led Kaiser Wilhelm to give up his throne. Meanwhile, on the Eastern Front, General Andranik's troops carried out a surprise offensive, defeating the Turks in the Ararat region. This battle was decisive. The Allies won the war.

Following their victory, the peace agreement was signed on November 11, 1918. Loud cheers, singing and much celebration echoed in the distance near the spot where the Armenian flag waved over Mount Ararat.

At the end of the war, after the demobilization of Armen's regiment, he received an unexpected monetary bonus, assets made available to the army through the generous support of America and other nations. Armen viewed the extra money as a blessing from Heaven, a means to start over. Still, he had mixed feelings. After serving in the military, Armen felt more alone than ever, and now he was also jobless. The revenge he'd desired had left him empty. Four years had passed since the death of his family, but he continued to grieve for them. He had made a few friends while in the military, and then he had watched them die as well. Time and again, Armen had miraculously survived imminent death, but outliving friends and loved ones resulted in a very lonely existence. Armen reasoned that it was possible to go back to camel-driving with Mr. Soulehmen, but such a life no longer appealed to him. In some unexplainable way, Armen sensed that God was leading him in a new direction, although he had no idea where that might be. Nevertheless, he decided to put his doubts aside and attempt to follow God's leading.

For the first time in years, Armen could travel freely, without the constant threat of an enemy assault. For that reason, he decided to spend some leisurely time on the road before seeking employment. Now eighteen-years-old, Armen made his way from Van through Bitlis, Diarbekr, Ufra, Adana and Tarsus. In Ufra he joined the many tourists visiting a certain cave believed to be the birthplace of the patriarch Abraham. Then in Tarsus, an important metropolis during the Roman era, he saw many sites, including places that commemorated the Apostle Paul and early Christianity. During this time, Armen discovered the earliest settlers in the region could be traced back to the Hittites mentioned in the Old Testament; many believed the Armenians descended from this ancient tribe.

After touring those cities, Armen boarded a ship for Constantinople. The travel route took him down the Dardanelle's Strait, which had been closed during the war. There were plenty of ships in the water that day; three of them had the same beautiful flag waving in the sunlight. Armen was surprised by his sudden, intense feelings that surged at the sight of the strange flag. Stopping a nearby passenger, he asked, "Excuse me, Sir? What nation is represented by the red, white and blue flag?"

"That's the banner of the United States of America," the passenger replied.

Armen marveled as he watched the beautiful flags flutter in the breeze. His heart had stirred within him each time he'd heard mention of this country. Just as Armen had sensed God was leading him in a new direction, he now felt a longing for a country that he did not know. He was sure this flag somehow represented the calling of God upon his future.

Arriving near the city of Constantinople, Armen's ship entered the Golden Horn harbor—a deep, horn-shaped inlet which separated the city into two parts. It divided Asia from Europe and connected the Black Sea with the Sea of Marmora. This spot joined another strait called Bosphorus; the location was known as Seraglio Point. Like Rome, the city of Constantinople was built on a series of seven hills topped with magnificent mosques and palaces. In the distance, Armen saw the slender minarets and broad domes overlooking the bay. Surrounding both sides of the water were charming villages and beautiful gardens. Above them, the mosque of Sultan Achmet and others were breathtaking. Armen was fascinated by their brilliant architectural design. At the main entrance was another magnificent sight: a large and lofty gate known as Bab Humayum (the door of the Sublime Porte). It was a massive stone gate with a central arch leading to the high-domed passage.

Day after day Armen explored the magnificent city, determined to experience all of its wonders. Constantinople was originally developed by the Greeks who named the territory Byzantium. Later, it became part of the Roman Empire and was reconstructed under the rule of Emperor Constantine, who eventually moved his capital there. When the city became severely weakened by constant enemy invasions, it was finally overtaken in 1453 by the Ottoman Empire.

Armen greatly enjoyed his time exploring the city, but before long his money began to dwindle. Finding employment was not an easy task; when it began to look like he would never find work, Armen prayed and asked God to provide. Shortly after this, Armen was offered a position at a coffee shop run by a Turk. It was not the most comfortable situation, nevertheless, he was grateful the man had hired him.

Armen's new job was very fast-paced. Armen soon learned there were about forty different ways to prepare Turkish coffee. Diverse customers frequented the shop: businessmen, military personnel, tourists and even fortune tellers. After work or dinner, the locals came in to socialize with friends and play table games.

As the days passed, Armen's longing for America grew stronger. He began to view his job not only as a way to survive but as a means to reach the United States of America. He resolved to save every penny toward that goal.

seventeen

"But as it is written, Eye hath not seen, nor ear heard, neither have entered into the heart of man, the things which God hath prepared for them that love him. But God hath revealed them unto us by his Spirit: for the Spirit searcheth all things, yea, the deep things of God." 1 Corinthians 2:9-10

Armen had been working in the coffee shop for months. With the low wages he earned, his dream of going to America was fading. He could barely afford what he needed to survive, let alone a costly trip across the ocean. Seeing no hope for advancement, he began to wonder if all his hard work was for nothing. Even though God had done miracles in his life before, he felt abandoned.

Then one day, while he was on break, Armen decided to go through the stack of international newspapers that his boss kept on hand for the tourists. One paper—an Armenian publication from Boston, Massachusetts—instantly caught his attention. He was turning the pages when suddenly, much to his surprise, there was his father's name in bold print:

Will the survivors of Hagop Arakelian, late of Nevsher, Turkey, please get in touch with Mamas Casapian, 747 E. 14th Street, New York City, New York, USA.

Armen's heart raced, and he could barely breathe. He thought perhaps his eyes were playing tricks on him, so he read and reread the small ad. Could it really be possible? He kept reading the same words over and over again until he was convinced it was real. This Mr. Casapian was indeed his uncle! That night Armen was too excited to sleep. His emotions ranged from anticipation to despair. He could claim kinship with his father's family, but he had very little hope of ever securing the money necessary to be reunited with his relatives. Hour after long hour he lay in bed thinking, trying to figure out a way to make it possible. But no feasible plan came to him.

Early the next morning, Armen visited the only friend he had in Constantinople—an old shoe cobbler. The old man helped him to write a letter to Mr. Casapian. With great anticipation, and a fair amount of fear, Armen sent the letter off to America.

The mail traveled very slowly, especially because of the recent war. Therefore, Armen attempted to wait patiently as the next three months drug along without a response from Mr. Casapian. Armen went about his daily chores, feeling himself in a fog. During this time of waiting, he knew in his mind that the Lord was in control of his future, but he had great difficulty convincing himself that God's plans would be for his good. His dear mother would have told him to be patient and surrender to God's will, but his feelings resisted. He had endured so much pain and loss, *all while the Lord was in control of his future* . . . As he allowed these faithless thoughts to dominate his mind more and more, his depression grew heavier; it affected his job, as well as every area of his life. The only time he seemed to have energy was when the foreign mail arrived. Yet with every passing day without a letter of response, Armen's suffocating disappointment increased.

Finally one day, a letter arrived from America; it was addressed to Armen. His hands trembled as he tore the envelope open. When he read his uncle's note, tears swelled in his eyes. Not only was this Mr. Casapian truly his uncle, he was also offering to pay for Armen's trip to America! All Armen had to do was send a photo and written documentation to verify his identity. Then the money would be wired by Mr. Casapian.

Once again, the Lord had proven that His plans far exceeded anything Armen could have imagined. Armen was humbled and greatly ashamed of his faithless attitude. God had continually proven to be kind and merciful, even to a young man who did not deserve His goodness.

eighteen

"O give thanks unto the Lord; for he is good; for his mercy en-dureth for ever." 1 Chronicles 16:34

Without any time wasted, Armen gathered the information and sent it to his uncle, Mr. Casapian. Another long wait followed. In time a second letter arrived stating that one-hundred and sixty-five dollars had been cabled to the Ottoman Bank in Constantinople. It was enough to purchase Armen's passport and ticket. Meanwhile, Mr. Casapian waited to receive the passenger information, including the name of the ocean liner and the date and time of his nephew's arrival.

When Armen arrived at the passport building, there were many Armenians in line ahead of him. Apparently, he was not the only one who wanted to travel to America! So he camped on the doorstep of the office. Once again, there was nothing he could do but wait. Finally, after much pleading and a lot of red tape, he was able to secure his passport.

At last, the day arrived. It was June 3, 1920. Armen was proudly dressed in a new suit which the salesman had convinced him was the best in New York fashion. He left Constantinople in style and traveled by boat to Marseilles; from there, he took the train to Cherbourg where he boarded the passenger liner, *Lafayette*. Against incredible odds, Armen's dream of going to America was about to become reality.

Shortly after his ship set sail, Armen's joy suddenly turned into a strange feeling in his stomach. Slouched in a corner, he was so sick his fine clothes no longer mattered. One of the passengers, Mrs. Charvusian, took a liking to Armen and mothered him like he was her own son. Mr. and Mrs. Charvusian and their children had come from a village named Everek. Armen was glad for their company, although being in their presence made him long for the siblings and parents he had lost.

Another passenger, seeing Armen's persistent seasickness, told him a story, hoping it might cheer him. "Early in the evening," he said, "a man was on deck, close to the rail, when a friend spoke in a soothing voice. 'Never mind, you're going to feel better soon—the moon will be coming up and—'

'Oh no!' groaned the victim who had lost breakfast, lunch and dinner, 'Does that have to come up too?'"

Armen, slumped over with sea-sickness, was not able to fully appreciate the humor of the joke.

When the ship steamed into the New York harbor at last, Armen's enthusiasm returned. He joined his newfound friends, the Charvusians, in prayer as they thanked God for bringing them safely to this new country. He arrived at Ellis Island on July 26th, 1920. The weather was extremely hot and sticky that day, but Armen hardly noticed. Leaning upon the rails beside the Charvusian family, Armen gazed about, wide-eyed, and marveled at the beauty of his new country. With much joy, Armen proclaimed loudly, "I am glad to become an American! I wish also to have an American name, therefore, I shall be called by my middle name: John!" The Charvusians cheered in agreement. Then Armen John Arakelian threw his oriental sleeping mat overboard as a sign of his willingness to let go of the past in exchange for a new life in America.

However, entering New York City proved to be even more difficult than leaving Constantinople. Armen John waited for what seemed like an eternity. He reasoned that at least he was in America; this helped him to wait patiently. And then, at last, he heard someone calling his name:

"Armen John Arakelian!"

Rushing forward, he was informed that, in order to be admitted to the United States, he had to pass a physical exam to confirm that his health was excellent. Armen John's joy and enthusiasm suddenly turned to dread. He feared the physical rigors of the previous year's captivity, starvation and then war, would now doom him to be rejected by this new country. He struggled to calm his pounding heart and breathe normally as his examination began. Moments later, when he received a nod of approval, Armen John thanked God silently, but with great fervor. He had passed!!! Then, as a matter of formality, he was asked to read the scripture of John 1:6 from the Armenian Bible to prove that he could read. Clearing his throat, Armen John read:

"There was a man sent from God, whose name was John."

After reading, he was given permission to continue on. As he moved forward in line, John pondered the profound symbolism that the *Word of God*, for which he suffered so acutely in his own country, should now be the ticket of his admittance to his country of adoption.

John's thoughts were interrupted when he saw a distinguished looking gentleman standing in the doorway. The man was holding a picture of John and waving his hand. John hurried over to greet his uncle, Mr. Casapian. Together the two men walked away from the immigration building into the hustle and bustle of a New York City street.

John had never seen high buildings before. The city looked like an imaginary place from a fairy tale. But when he saw the crowds of people rushing around, he was reminded of the multitudes in Turkey crowded together and marched through the desert. He panicked and ran ahead of his uncle, looking for a place of safety. Mr. Casapian understood his fears. Speaking in a calm voice, he was able to put John's mind at ease before they headed homeward on the subway.

When they entered his uncle's home, John was fascinated by the unusual décor of spring bottom chairs, strange springy beds high off the floor, a table with legs, dish sets.

and silverware—which he had no idea how to use. Yet he was most intrigued by the portraits of two men hanging on the wall of Mr. Casapian's study. Curiosity got the best of him, so he asked his uncle, "Are these men your friends?"

Mr. Casapian laughed. "They are very good friends," he answered. Then he introduced John to the biographies of George Washington and Abraham Lincoln, which were written in Armenian. Before long, Armen John Arakelian began studying the history of his new country. During the first week in New York, Mr. and Mrs. Casapian took John on a sightseeing tour of the city. They visited Grant's tomb as well as several libraries and museums. John's most thrilling experience was climbing to the top of the Statue of Liberty; it was especially significant to him because he understood firsthand what it meant to long to live in a free world. One particular feature on the monument—the broken chains around the statue's feet— were a vivid reminder of his deliverance from tyranny to liberty.

After sightseeing, the Casapians treated John to dinner at one of their favorite restaurants. His mouth watered when he saw the delicious meal the waiter set in front of him—perfectly browned chicken with a medley of fresh vegetables. But he had not yet mastered the use of a fork and knife. Therefore, his chicken flung into the air and landed on the floor near the table next to them. His face turned red, and he wished for the wide open spaces of the desert. Everyone else, however, seemed to find the incident entertaining. Trying to adjust to a new way of life was difficult, but he soon learned to laugh at his mistakes and simply try to do better next time. This new attitude seemed to work.

Within time John Arakelian began attending classes. It was here that a teacher brought something to his attention that he'd been unaware of: he had a habit of walking with his head turned half-way to the rear as if he were antici-pating an attack from behind. "Keep your head up and your shoulders back, my boy," she said. "John Arakelian, you are just as free as the air you breathe, as long as you do what's right!" Afterward, John determined to try to walk as if he were free and were not being followed. Still, there were many days when he did not feel as free as the air; his grief and memories haunted him.

nineteen

"And we know that all things work together for good to them that love God, to them who are the called according to his purpose. For whom he did foreknow, he also did predestinate to be conformed to the image of his Son, that he might be the first-born among many brethren." Romans 8:28-29

As John gradually adjusted to his new country, he learned that he wasn't the only one permanently altered by the war. The Great War had changed the entire world; around nine million soldiers and six million civilians had died worldwide. Although it hadn't touched American soil, the war greatly impacted American lives as well as those in countries across the sea. The American dead numbered 115,000, over half of them from disease during wartime. Many soldiers who survived and returned were crippled in both body and mind. Having lived through extreme horror and violence, like John Arakelian, they were hardened, suspicious and unhappy.

However, John found that when he began attending weekly services at the Armenian church on Twenty-Seventh Street and Third Avenue, much of the oppressive darkness that plagued him lifted. There he met other young adults and was reassured to see that some of them were also adjusting to a new lifestyle, in addition to battling the lasting effects of tragedy and horror.

One day in March of 1921, John and his friends stopped to buy a newspaper on their way home from church. The headlines read that Talaat Pasha had been murdered — Talaat was responsible for the deportation of thousands of Armenians. Following the surrender of the Ottoman Empire, in 1918, the Three Pashas — Talaat, Enver and Djemal — fled to Germany, where they were given protection. The article explained that a young man (whose mother had been slaughtered) sought revenge, shooting Talaat openly in the street of Berlin, Germany. Additionally, there were rumors that Enver Pasha had been killed by the Russians, and Djemal Pasha had been murdered in Tiflis.

John wasn't sure how to receive the news. He remembered Talaat Pasha — his orders had turned a multitude of cherished babies and children into a burning pile of rubble. John found himself thinking (and being somewhat comforted by the fact) that these men would now face judgment and be repaid for the suffering they had inflicted on others.

All around him, John's bitterness was reflected in the words and faces of the people he met. The war had been expected to end all wars — to make the world safe for democracy and bring liberty and prosperity to all. The war had brought new jobs and sudden prosperity to the country. But when the war ended, the jobs and prosperity ended abruptly.

The leaders of the United States, busy drafting terms of peace, had not considered how to transition the country into peacetime. The day after the armistice was signed, government officials called suppliers to cancel contracts for four billion dollars' worth of war supplies. Factories shut down overnight, and nine million American workers lost their jobs. Meanwhile, the government gave a railway ticket home, and sixty dollars apiece, to the four million men who served in the armed forces. They came home heroes, but no jobs awaited them. Many of them were now crippled, but no provisions had been made to help them support their families or to readjust to civilian life. As if that weren't enough, each day scores of immigrants poured into the United States of America from the war-ravaged eastern countries. They sought refuge and, of course, jobs. Within this context, Americans were disillusioned and entered a time of bitterness; they rejected the morals and values of previous generations and searched for meaning through looser morals and more entertainment.

Despite the obvious upheaval in the society around him, John remained thankful for his new country. As the months went by, he became more comfortable, especially when his diligent study of English paid off, and he could converse fluently with anyone he met. Then, despite widespread unemployment, John's uncle found a job for him in a tailor shop—for which he was extremely grateful. John worked during the day and went to school at night. But on Sundays he spent most of the day in church.

As John's life settled into a busy routine, his top priority was to apply for United States citizenship. This undertaking required a lot of study in American history. When he was called for his first government examination, he was delighted to see all the questions focusing on the life and ideals of the emancipator Abraham Lincoln. He breezed through the test without any difficulty.

One day, when he had some free time, John and several of his friends spent the afternoon at Van Courtland Park. John was surprised to see Mrs. Charvusian and her husband there—they were the family who had looked after him while he was seasick on the ship *Lafayette*. Although it seemed like a chance meeting, John didn't believe in coincidences; God brought people into his life for a reason. The Charvusians eventually invited John to stay at their home, which was conveniently located near the tailor shop where he was employed.

John continued to work hard, and the horrific events of his past began to fade away. People were attracted to John's flashing smile and quaint speech. He made many friends and had many invitations to go to the beach or movies, whenever he wasn't busy with work or school. His business connections were profitable, and his bank account was rapidly growing. John felt that he was sitting on top of the world.

But then one evening, when John had plans to go out, he was stopped short at the front door; he heard someone weeping. Turning back inside the home of his host family, he found Mrs. Charvusian sobbing over an opened letter she had received from her widowed sister, in the Turkish village of Everek. Mrs. Charvusian's sister wrote that the Turks had learned of her beautiful eighteen-year-old daughter, Anneza Ohanian. Now she was to be seized for the harem. Anneza's mother was frantic; in desperation she had written to her sister in America, begging her to save her daughter. Although the Great World War was supposed to have ended such persecution, the actions of the Turks had changed very little, especially in the smaller towns of the interior. After reading the letter to John, Mrs. Charvusian clutched it to her chest and resumed crying; she couldn't help her niece.

John was deeply troubled by the news—it brought to mind all of the things he usually dared not to think about. Like the rest of American society, he had been filling his mind with higher learning and his days and nights with fun and exciting activities—all in an effort to forget the past. But his past was still this girl's future; Armen John Arakelian was overcome by the realization that, while he enjoyed a new life of freedom and prosperity, suffering was still ongoing for others. Memories of his mother returned to him, his dear mother whose faith and love had not wavered even as she was drug to her death. His mind also filled with the faces of his lovely sister Parease and the crudely tattooed face of brave Zartar.

Canceling all plans to go out, John talked with Mrs. Charvusian until the wee hours of the morning. He found paper and scribbled out a feasible plan for the escape of Mrs. Charvusian's niece. Anneza would travel in disguise, wearing fine black satin clothes and the veil worn by prominent Turkish ladies of her town. Then, as customary for women, she would travel by horseback to the railroad in Ulu Kerslaugh; there she would board a train to Konieth and finally arrive in Marseilles, France, where John would be waiting to deliver her to the Armenian Relief Association. A short time earlier, John had learned that a cousin of his was living in a suburb of Marseilles, France. Now he was reasonably confident that he could lodge with his cousin. John assured Mrs. Ohanian that, if at any time her daughter's life was threatened, he was prepared to go all the way to Turkey to rescue her.

In the morning, Mrs. Charvusian helped John send a letter to Mrs. Ohanian presenting his idea. In time a reply came from Mrs. Ohanian. She gladly accepted John's offer, and her daughter Anneza was willing to follow his instructions. Her son Garabed had secretly secured an acceptable disguise for his sister; now they would await John's directives and details for Anneza's departure. "But please do hurry," begged Mrs. Ohanian. "Time is running out."

twenty

Anneza

"My son, forget not my law; but let thine heart keep my commandments: for length of days, and long life, and peace, shall they add to thee. Let not mercy and truth forsake thee: bind them about thy neck; write them upon the table of thine heart: So shalt thou find favour and good understanding in the sight of God and man. Trust in the Lord with all thine heart; and lean not unto thine own understanding. In all thy ways acknowledge him, and he shall direct thy paths. Be not wise in thine own eyes: fear the Lord, and depart from evil."
Proverbs 3:1-7

At the end of the Great War, the Armenian flag was resurrected. It had been hidden under almost six centuries of Turkish rule. Now the beloved flag floated to the breeze over Mount Ararat, proclaiming new-born freedom. However, few Armenians remained to see it.

The Armenian people—whose first chief was Haik, the son of Togarmah, the son of Gomar, the son of Japheth, the son of Noah—had suffered an incredible blow. The Ottomans and Young Turk Revolutionaries had killed millions of Armenians. When they first came to power, the Young Turks had appeared to be enacting democratic reforms. Their genocidal sweep of the Christian Armenian population was eventually revealed—but it was too late. They had forcefully recruited unsuspecting Armenian young men into the military, made them "non-combatant" soldiers (taking away their weapons) and then marched them into the woods and deserts, where they were ambushed and massacred.

With the Armenian young men gone, their cities and villages were defenseless. Nearly two million old men, women and children were then herded into the desert, thrown off cliffs, or burnt alive. Entire Armenian communities were deported to the deserts of Syria and Mesopotamia, where hundreds of thousands were killed or starved to death. The Armenian cities of Kharpert, Van and Ani were leveled.

At the end of the war, upon the collapse of Turkey, the Triumvirate—Enver, Talaat and Djemal—had fled to Germany. Mehmet Reshad, the old Sultan, died in July, 1918, and Vahededdin, the heir-apparent, had ascended the throne as Mohammed VI. The war was over, the Armistice signed—the Armenian flag was flying—but confusion, oppression and unrest continued to surge throughout the land.

When word of the peace agreement reached Anneza and her family, they returned to Everek. There they found very little that resembled the village of their youth. As the weary Ohanian family trudged into their village, no cries of welcome greeted them. Most of the Armenian families were gone and their houses leveled. Little Serapi, weak from lack of food, rode atop Garabed's shoulders as they passed the site where the missionaries had once been building the boy's orphanage. The buildings had been burned and the wall reduced to rubble. Never again would boys sit atop the wall, saluting them with a cheerful, "Hoshgelden!"

Back in Everek, the Ohanians found their home had also been destroyed. In fact, Anneza's aunt and uncle's home was one of the only Armenian cottages still standing. Because the Charvusians had already left the region, first seeking refuge in nearby Hadjin and then immigrating to America, the nearly-starved Ohanians took temporary shelter in their empty home.

About the time the Ohanians ventured back to Everek, the missionaries Mrs. Eby and Mrs. Bredemus sailed from North America to return to Turkey after the war. They needed to know the fate of the orphans and the orphanages they had helped to build. Arriving in Hadjin, they found the girl's orphanage had been burned and the orphans scattered. But the missionaries' home still stood, so they moved in. Very soon, a company of orphans gathered around them again, including some orphan boys who had escaped the chaos in nearby Everek. Prior to the war, the population of Hadjin consisted of only about sixty Turkish families (besides the officials and the standing army), out of a total population of twenty-thousand. Therefore, Hadjin was a refuge for many Armenians. However, by 1920 there were only ten-thousand Armenians left in Hadjin; before a year had passed, Hadjin was besieged by the Nationalists (Kemalists). After almost three months of siege, the Canadian and American missionaries escaped from the city while it was yet under siege. Of the ten-thousand Armenians living in Hadjin at this time, only 480 survived.

While unrest in their region continued to simmer, Anneza and her family prayed fervently, and God continued to provide. Later, Vartuhi was greatly encouraged when she received correspondence from her sister, Mrs. Charvusian, informing her that her family had safely settled in America. And, although dangers persisted, Anneza found herself growing somewhat less fearful as the days went by.

Shortly after arriving at the home of her aunt and uncle, Anneza had discovered something that changed her life: she found an Armenian Bible—a gift from the Biblewomen of the orphanage. During her years of hiding during the war, Anneza had poured out many words to God. Now she gratefully received His words to her! Her spirit and soul were greatly strengthened by what she read. Often she prayed for blessings upon the missionaries who had crossed the ocean and risked their lives to share God's love and word with her people.

By the year 1921, things were not much improved for the few Armenians left in Turkey. Jobs and food were scarce for Armenian men, and young Armenian women and girls were still routinely kidnapped. Despite all attempts to keep the Ohanian girls hidden, the Turkish men of the region eventually discovered their existence.

And so it was, early one morning after another sleepless night, Vartuhi called Anneza to sit before her and listen.

"I have decided something, and I will not change my mind," Vartuhi said.

Anneza waited, growing nervous, knowing by the look upon her mother's face that she would not like what she heard. Behind her, Anneza heard her sister Serapi rise from her sleeping mat and tiptoe down the hall toward them.

With tears in her eyes, Vartuhi continued, "I have written to my sister in America; I am sending you to her."

"Without you? Without Sera?" Anneza asked, her heart suddenly racing. How could she leave her family? How could Anneza, who had rarely been outside of a hiding spot for years, travel to America—alone?

"We will lose you soon, Anneza," Vartuhi replied, shaking her head in defeat. "One way or another, we will lose you soon."

Anneza wanted to argue, but her mother was correct. Holding back her many arguments, instead she nodded. "How will she get me out of Turkey? I cannot see any possible way."

Shrugging, Vartuhi replied, "God will determine how. I have prayed and *I have let you go.*"

Just then, Serapi rushed in to the room, sobbing. "But I don't want you to leave me!" she cried. "I have *not* let you go, Anneza!"

Anneza took her weeping little sister into her arms and comforted her. That day she began reading to Serapi from her treasured Bible. Afterward, as the days of waiting for a reply from Mrs. Charvusian passed, again and again the girls returned to a certain passage:

"The Lord himself will lead you and be with you. He will not fail you or abandon you, so do not lose courage or be afraid."

This passage became their anchor. Therefore, when at long last Vartuhi received a letter from her sister, along with the letter from young Armen John Arakelian, Anneza felt a burst of hope. Although it was a dangerous plan, outlined by a total stranger, in a scribbled note from the other side of the world, Anneza accepted it as an answer to her constant prayers.

Holding Serapi's hand, Anneza bowed her head and spoke aloud, "Merciful Father God, in the name of Jesus, if you will deliver me, please also provide a way of escape for my sister, Serapi; she too is afflicted with beauty and will mature soon. Amen."

twenty-one

John

"... he giveth to all life, and breath, and all things; and hath made of one blood all nations of men for to dwell on all the face of the earth, and hath determined the times before appointed, and the bounds of their habitation; that they should seek the Lord, if haply they might feel after him, and find him, though he be not far from every one of us: For in him we live, and move, and have our being ..." Acts 17:25b-28a

After forwarding Anneza's detailed traveling instructions to the Ohanians, John sailed from New York on the *La France*. This time he enjoyed every minute of his voyage.

In France, his cousin Petros met him at the ship. "John, you are crazy!" Petros said at once. "Who rushes to the rescue of a girl he has never seen and knows nothing about? Are you so desperate to find a wife?" Petros looked at him expectantly.

Taken aback, John retorted, "Marriage has never entered my mind!" As they left the docks, John reminded Petros of the fate of his dear sister Parease. "Petros, don't you see? This girl could have been my sister. But suppose someone had come to her aid!?" John said. "How could I ever be happy again if I disregard an opportunity to help a girl in a like situation?"

Beginning to understand, Petros agreed. "Forgive my hasty judgment, Cousin," he said.

"Look," John continued, "I want to show you something." Baring his arm, John displayed Zartar's tattoo marks. "Here is another reason why I cannot refuse to help this girl," he said. John told Petros how Zartar had saved his life in the desert and risked her life to help him escape. From that time on, both Petros and his wife were eager to help little Miss Anneza Ohanian flee from life in a Turkish harem.

Two days after John's arrival in Marseilles, France, a telegram arrived stating that Anneza had successfully left Turkey.

Shortly after that, John received a letter from Mrs. Ohanian describing Anneza's departure. Following John's plan, both mother and daughter had discarded their usual Armenian attire, arrayed themselves in the fine black satin costume and voluminous veils of quality Turkish ladies, then taken fast Arabian horses to the railroad at Ulu Kerslaugh, where Anneza was to board a train for Konieth. Mrs. Ohanian's letter informed him that, before Anneza boarded the train, she had prayed once more for her daughter, asking God to protect her and carry her to a land where she would be safe from persecution. Afterward, Vartuhi said goodbye and put her on the train for Konieth, where she would exchange for Beirut.

Three long months passed, and neither John nor the Ohanians received word from Anneza. It was far past the date that she should have arrived in France. John was quite worried as he wondered what on earth kept her from coming. Her unexplained delay would have caused great anxiety had she been an eighteen-year-old American girl traveling alone. But for a little Armenian girl not to arrive on time—a girl who had not experienced any form of freedom or independence—this was a catastrophe. Having gone so far in the matter, John felt duty-bound to see it through. Yet three precious months were gone already! His absence from America could not exceed a six month's period, otherwise he forfeited his first papers and could only return to America under the Immigration Law once more. He wanted to help this poor girl, but he did not want to forfeit his citizenship papers. Nevertheless, he knew what he would choose; he would not leave France until Miss Ohanian's safety was settled.

When at last John received an explanatory letter from Anneza, he was only partially reassured. She wrote in great fear and dismay; upon reaching Beirut she was told that the quota was filled; she would need to wait her turn. It would be at least one year and a half before she would be allowed to leave for France.

Approaching Petros with the letter, John read it to him with great disgust and frustration. How could Miss Ohanian survive a year and a half waiting to leave Beirut?!

"John, I believe I can help you, if you're willing to spend a little money," Petros answered thoughtfully.

"I don't care about the money! If you know of a way, let's get on with it," John answered.

Accordingly, Petros called on a certain French Government Attaché. In the end it cost John over thirteen hundred francs for authentic release papers, which were forwarded to Anneza by airmail. These she was to deliver to the French Consul at Beirut to procure her release.

In less than three weeks, John was at the dock waiting to meet little Miss Ohanian. It proved quite a task to locate her. Up and down the dock John and Petros went, calling out, "Miss Ohanian!? Anneza Ohanian!" There was no response.

Just as they concluded that she'd been delayed once again, one of her fellow passengers, an elderly lady, heard them calling out. "I know who you're seeking," she said. They followed the old woman far back into the shadows. Here, at last, they found Anneza, hiding beneath her Turkish veil, bewildered and speechless.

twenty-two

"Hereby perceive we the love of God, because he laid down his life for us: and we ought to lay down our lives for the brethren. But whoso hath this world's good, and seeth his brother have need, and shutteth up his bowels of compassion from him, how dwelleth the love of God in him?" 1 John 3:16-17

Gently, John and Petros led Miss Ohanian down the gangplank and into a taxi. She was silent and appeared to be trembling. It was not until they turned her over to Petros' wife that the floodgates opened, and they at last heard her voice.

After her first shyness wore away, John found it an easy task to get acquainted with Miss Ohanian. She bloomed like a flower in the friendly atmosphere and security of his cousin's home. Putting first things first, he spoke with Miss Ohanian of her future; he had decided that the best plan to follow would be what he had first suggested, namely, introducing her to the Armenian Relief in Paris. He felt his responsibility would not end until she was satisfactorily settled and cared for so he could report both to her mother and her aunt, Mrs. Charvusian, with whom he lived.

However, it is said that no city in the world fascinates like Paris—John reasoned that it would not be reasonable to leave the city without sightseeing first. When John asked Miss Ohanian her opinion, she agreed.

To see Paris with so charming a companion as Miss Ohanian was an unexpected pleasure for John. Smartly gowned in Paris clothes, she was lovely, and her dark eyes seemed to glow with appreciation for all the beauty around her. They shared many of the same interests, and their conversation flowed effortlessly. After visiting the famous historical sites, they spent time at the Cafe de la Paix, watching the rest of the world go by. In the presence of Miss Ohanian, John felt he was getting a taste of the joy he'd lost when his sister, brothers and parents were taken from him so suddenly and violently.

The week of sight-seeing was certainly a pleasant interlude. Some days Petros and his wife accompanied John and Miss Ohanian. In the evenings Anneza played her lyre softly for the group; it was one of the few things she had brought with her. John enjoyed her music greatly.

At the end of the week, John sat in Petros' pretty little garden one evening, enjoying the dewy fragrance of the flowers in the moonlight. It was time for him to be getting back to America, so he was taking account of himself. In so doing, he'd begun to realize the pattern of his life had changed, and, quite frankly, he was startled. Just a few months before, he'd had his future outlined. His intention had been to embrace higher education; he built his bank account with that thought in mind, for he was thirsty for knowledge. With it he intended to conquer life! But then, in the twinkling of an eye—a split second overhearing

Mrs. Charvusian weeping over a letter from home—John's plans had all changed. Instead of pursuing his dreams, he had felt bound to save a girl from the suffering of which his sister had not been saved.

Now, as he took account of the past few months, he reminded himself that it had been worthwhile. But it was time to return to America. It was time to get back on track, to follow his plans—to find new worlds to conquer! Yet something held him back.

Why, already the girl was like a sister—that was the problem! How did one deliver a *sister* to the Armenian Relief Association and then walk away? John's feelings and thoughts confused him. Jumping to his feet, he paced the garden walk in an unusual fit of agitation, his mind a jumble of new, strange thoughts. Was she truly like a sister? He tried to reason out this sudden, chaotic state of mind; but reason had apparently left him. Instead, he found himself wanting to do several different things at once and immediately discarding all of them.

Again he insisted that his feelings and thoughts fall in line; his plans were made! Tomorrow he would take Miss Ohanian to the Armenian Relief Association, and, as soon as she was settled, he would sail back to America, leaving her . . . behind—all alone. She would be frightened again and lonely . . . until she met someone, for undoubtedly the girl was lovely; she would attract suitors. And . . . she would marry—someone. Suddenly, John's gaze quickened, for the girl had just emerged from the shadows and was walking toward him, with a smile on her lips. It was instantly borne in upon him that she was beautiful. Not only beautiful, as his sister Parease had been, but uncommonly, incredibly, brilliantly so. Strange, he hadn't noticed before . . .

Anneza Ohanian lifted her large, trustful, brown eyes to meet his glance, and there came a sudden flash of illumination: he had to convince her to become *his* wife!

twenty-three

"O the depth of the riches both of the wisdom and knowledge of God! how unsearchable are his judgments, and his ways past finding out!" Romans 11:33

John and Anneza were married almost at once. But what should have been a purely joyous occasion was overshadowed by a great concern; Armen John Arakelian could not take his wife home with him, for he was not yet a naturalized citizen of America. Anneza would either have to go through all the red-tape of entering under the Immigrant Law or wait until John received his final citizenship papers. Weighing their difficult options, the couple finally decided that Anneza would wait in Paris as the guest of Petros and his wife. After John was an American citizen, she would have no difficulty coming in as his wife.

Once more John boarded a huge ocean liner bound for America, now trusting his relatives to look after his lonely little bride during the time of exile. As the shore-line of France receded, John caught the last flutter of a wisp of a handkerchief; with that, he straightway began to plan for the home he would to prepare for his wife.

The news of John and Anneza's marriage caused much rejoicing in the Charvusian household, and he was welcomed home as one of the family. His life took on new beauty and meaning, having someone to work and plan for. In anticipation of his reunion with his bride, John purchased a small, cozy home. Many happy hours went into the furnishing of it. He shopped around until he found just the things which appealed to his sense of the beautiful; at the same time, he did not overlook comfort, for he wanted a real home.

However, John and Anneza's future together depended upon John obtaining citizenship—which wasn't an entirely worry-free process for an Armenian. Armen John Arakelian, like all Armenians, had always considered himself an *Oriental*. In fact, Armenia was geographically thought of as part of Asia. Yet only "White" races were eligible for United States citizenship—and the courts took special time and effort to affirm that Asians, especially, were to be excluded.

Numerous immigrants recalled the sight of the Statute of Liberty as their ship approached Ellis Island, the gate to the *Promised Land*. For many refugees, including John, it was one of the most beautiful sights they'd ever seen. The inscription on the statue read:

```
      "Give me your tired, your poor, your huddled
   masses yearning to breathe free; the wretched
    refuse of your teeming shore. Send these, the
 homeless, tempest-tossed to me. I lift my lamp
                beside the golden door!"
```

America was known as a welcoming land for the immigrant, a nation comprised of newcomers absorbed as citizens in the giant melting pot. However, the U.S.

Immigration Service, specifically the Ellis Island officials, had created a "List of Races or Peoples" to help them classify arrivals at their immigration station. When an immigrant came to early twentieth-century America, his or her ability to become a citizen was dependent on this list—and there were only two classifications that really mattered: *White*, or *non-White*.

Most of the people classified as White were of Anglo-Saxon descent. However, Armenian immigrants were the ultimate "in-between" people. They were geographically between Europe and Asia and racially between Caucasian and Mongolian—in other words, between *White* and *Yellow*. Even their language (after six centuries of domination) was a mixture of common Turkish and traditional Armenian words, making them even harder to define. Nevertheless, the Armenians had made it onto the "White list" partly due to the testimony of an anthropologist who swore that the Armenians were not Mongolian. But their future was not guaranteed; the courts had concluded, multiple times, that "White" was to be determined not by science but by "common understanding" of who was White and who was not. Unfortunately, common understanding varied from day to day and from person to person.

Such was the case when—while John was working on obtaining his citizenship, and Anneza was waiting for him in France—naturalization officers went to court and began questioning whether Armenians might actually be of the Mongolian race, therefore, racially ineligible for citizenship.

Meanwhile, John continued working toward his citizenship, despite the fact that his (and his bride's) future was far from certain. If the naturalization officers won their case, all Armenians previously awarded citizenship would lose it, and all Armenian property-holders in America would legally lose their properties. During this time, John penned many long letters to his young wife who waited for him in France. He didn't mention his worries but spoke fondly of the country that had taken him in. John and Anneza wrote also of their homeland, the continued plight of their people and the families they missed. And so a year of waiting passed.

Despite those who opposed an Armenians' right to naturalize, the day finally came when John was acknowledged as a citizen of the United States of America. He knew that it was by God's merciful hand that the flag he had loved, from the moment his eyes first rested upon it, was now his flag. He was nearly overwhelmed as he looked with awe upon his naturalization certificate. He had received in a few short years what poor, oppressed Armenia had struggled for centuries to attain, only to fail: Armen John Arakelian, an Armenian, was free! America had welcomed him just as he was—untaught, poor, unaccomplished and bowed and broken from tyranny and oppression. And, arguably, *not exactly White.*

John was free to worship the God of his fathers in peace and security. Life, at that great moment, stretched ahead of him like a noble avenue paved with gold. On either side grew trees rich in the fruit of opportunity and advantage; and above was the clear, blue sky after the storm—

where God, in his infinite goodness and love, had flung out His lovely and enduring rainbow of promise.

The day that Anneza was to arrive by ship, John looked their little home over for the last time. Assuring himself that he had overlooked nothing of necessity, he softly closed the door, made his way to a florist — where he ordered the first American flowers his wife would ever receive — and then rushed to the pier to meet the *Majestic*, on which would be his wife.

Of course, John was a little early. As the *Majestic* nosed her way around the dock, his eyes were glued on the maelstrom of motion and color above him on the gigantic liner. After what seemed an unbearable length of time, he finally spotted his young wife; it was a moment of exquisite happiness, thankfulness and of mixed emotions. He watched her reaction to the breath-taking skyline of New York and the Statue of Liberty welcoming her through a glamorous, silver fog. The glorious stars and stripes, floating to the breeze, were the crowning touch of beauty and color adorning that never-to-be-forgotten picture. John's eyes searched deeply the sparkling brown ones of the radiant-faced girl who had traveled so many miles to share his life and home. Would she like America? It was so large — a place of power; a place of wealth. But, in essence, America was a *people*. Though foreign born, John had become a son of this people, and now Anneza was a daughter.

Unlike the Anglo-Saxons, Orientals did not repress their emotions. Therefore, when the long-awaited moment came that John's bride was finally within arm's-reach, he momentarily put off his new American identity. In true Oriental fashion, John wept great tears of joy, very much unashamedly. Placing his lips near her ear, John spoke softly in their native tongue and in tones vibrating with the sheer joy of living. "My dear, we have trod the hot sands of the desert; we have endured the hardships of siege and war; we have tasted the bitterness of almost every known sorrow, but praise the Lord; He has brought us through them all; today we are American citizens reaching home."

twenty-four

Anneza

"Oh how great is thy goodness, which thou hast laid up for them that fear thee; which thou hast wrought for them that trust in thee before the sons of men!" Psalms 31:19

The Arakelian's modest home was located in a business district of Haddon Avenue (also called Main Street), the oldest road from Camden to Westmont, New Jersey. Below their home was a store-front where John opened a tailor shop and dry-cleaning business. For Anneza, life in America was incredibly good. But it was also, at times, overwhelming and dreadfully confusing. She marveled at the prosperity of her new life; she had all the food she could eat, an abundance of warm clothing, the most comfortable home she'd ever been inside and true companionship. From her first moment with John, he felt like family; his humor and kindness reminded her of her brothers; his protective nature of her beloved father. Armen John Arakelian was a precious gift from a gracious, loving God; her new homeland was an answer to prayer.

However, American society baffled Anneza. When she arrived in America the "roaring twenties" was still in full swing; it was a loud and sensuous era. Despite being known as a "Christian" nation, church attendance was very low, and things previously condemned by American society were now celebrated shamelessly. America enjoyed a booming economy during the Great War; afterward Americans continued to spend to the extreme — now using borrowed money. Signs of impending economic hardship seemed quite evident, but America's leaders assured everyone that the future was going to be even more glorious. "We see fifty years of prosperity ahead," they promised, "with two chickens in every pot and a car in every garage!"

As Anneza struggled to learn English, she came to realize that material goods and entertainment, such as boxing matches, dominated American conversation. Even in church the messages often contained little, if any, biblical teaching.

Anneza was grateful for the prosperity and freedom in America. But she found it hard to adjust to her new country. Besides, she had received grievous news from home; her mother had become ill and passed away, leaving young Serapi in the care of her older brothers. Believing their chances would be better in Istanbul, the little group had moved to the city and opened a barber shop there. Anneza and Serapi communicated by letter as often as possible, but hearing of their continued hardships only increased Anneza's longing to be with her siblings.

But then, in 1927, some of Anneza's homesickness was replaced with joy when she and John had their first child — a gentle-natured, dark-eyed, dark-haired girl. It was love at first sight for Anneza and John; they named their baby Agayne, after John's mother.

Anneza loved being a mother. But with each new thing baby Agayne learned to do, Anneza remembered teaching Serapi to do the same things. One cold, winter night, as Anneza and John lay down to sleep, Anneza began to weep. Sitting up, John turned on their small bedside lamp. "What is it?" he asked.

"The bed is so warm!" Anneza sobbed.

"The bed?" John inquired. "Then let's take the blankets down," he said. With that, he flung the thick blankets aside and smiled expectantly at his young wife. But Anneza continued to weep.

"My closets overflow with warm clothes; Agayne has two winter coats, and my stomach is full!" she cried.

"Anneza?" John asked. "Do you want another bureau for the baby and bigger closets?" John shook his head in confusion. "And less food?"

"No, John," Anneza replied, "my sister Serapi is hungry, and she's cold." Anneza sobbed. "I'm no longer there to keep her warm at night!"

Thereafter, John made sure that Anneza had the money to purchase warm clothes, blankets and needful things to send to her family. Several years later—in 1933—Anneza and John had their second child, whom they named Parease, in honor of John's sister. Parease was an adorable child with striking features, like her older sister Agayne. But Parease was more active, always looking for new things to explore, and easily acquiring bumps, bruises and scrapes for her mother to bandage.

For the Arakelians, it should have been a glorious time; their family was growing, they had a home, a successful business, friends and all the freedoms they had ever dreamed of. However, they continued to hear of trouble in their homeland; despite the diligent efforts of Anneza's brothers, it was not a safe place for a little girl with neither mother nor father. Anneza doubled her prayers and efforts to find a way for Serapi to come to America.

The Arakelians were not the only ones with worries at this time; the country that they loved, she who had taken them in, had entered very dark days. As Americans, the Arakelian's fate and future were now intertwined with that of their adoptive nation.

A few years earlier, in 1929, the stock market crashed, taking with it all hopes that American prosperity would return. Many people lost vast fortunes and, in response, some committed suicide. Thousands of banks went out of business, and in every town and city across the country stores and factories failed and closed their doors. In just three years the average American's income dropped 40 percent; by 1933 one-third of the U.S. working population was unemployed. When the value of farm products fell below transportation costs, farmers in the west—in an effort to improve prices—began burning their fields of crops and dumping milk on the ground. Prices did not improve as a result, but widespread hunger in the cities grew more dire.

That was only the beginning; in the years that followed, America was hit with severe drought, plagues of grass-hoppers and even a dust-storm that lasted for four years—spreading thick clouds of dust across the nation and leaving a previously fertile region of the country without any topsoil. In cities nationwide, men and wom-en sold apples on street corners and stood in breadlines. Teenagers left home and rode freight trains looking for jobs because their parents could no longer afford to feed them. Many people died of malnutrition, either unable to get food or unwilling to beg. Countless Americans be-came homeless; they built makeshift shacks out of scrap materials and slept under newspapers.

As one calamity after another assaulted their nation, many people claimed that God had abandoned America. But not John; he began to speak of his mother more often. He remembered how her faith had not wavered despite the cruelest of circumstances. He promised Anneza that he would try not to let discouragement grip him as it had in the past when he couldn't see evidence of God's blessings—though he wasn't sure how to stand strong when faced with such severe worries and fears.

While the churches did not grow in numbers during this time of trials—no great revival swept the nation—it be-came a time of sober reappraisal, for the church and for the Arakelians. Whereas church-going people of the 1920s were convinced that Christianity meant simply following the *Golden Rule*—treating others as one would wish to be treated—and that through friendliness and kindness the *Kingdom of God* was slowly being built in America, they now saw things differently. Suddenly, they were confronted with the stark reality that their dreams had failed. But through this failure, they discovered the truth: God had not forsaken America—He was chastising them, trying to wake them up. Across America many churches now began to take a good look at old doctrines they had earlier thrown out—such as sin, faith and justification.

One Sunday, John and Anneza listened to their pastor preach a message based on 2 Corinthians 5:17:

"Therefore, if any man be in Christ, he is a new creature: old things are passed away; behold, all things are become new."

"Friends," the pastor said, "this does not describe dead-faith as in 2 Timothy 2:17, but neither is it about self-improvement or doing countless good deeds. No, this speaks of an impossibility—a supernatural miracle: that upon surrendering my life to Christ, I might be truly born again, raised up as a brand new person and filled with a whole new Spirit—the living Spirit of God!

"This is not about faith based on convincing intellectual arguments, but rather of receiving a brand new mind—the very mind of Christ! Our battle is not one of following the rules by exerting our will-power, but of literally dying to our own selves, thereby allowing the divine power of the Holy Spirit to reign, to miraculously raise us up and move us to do His will—as His very own body, set free from the power of sin and death, now slaves to righteousness."

After church, John seemed deep in thought. Finally, just when Anneza was truly beginning to worry about his prolonged silence, he began to speak. "Anneza, there's never been anything supernatural about my faith. I fear I've been just what my mother made me promise not to be," he said.

When Anneza raised her brows in question, John continued, "Mother said that many people are merely religious; they do not know Christ, therefore, they do not truly know the Father. Anneza, I know *of Christ*. But I don't believe I actually *know Christ*—I certainly don't believe I have His mind nor His power reigning within me. I don't believe I've ever become a new creation."

twenty-five

"I beseech you therefore, brethren, by the mercies of God, that ye present your bodies a living sacrifice, holy, acceptable unto God, which is your reasonable service. And be not conformed to this world: but be ye transformed by the renewing of your mind, that ye may prove what is that good, and acceptable, and perfect, will of God." Romans 12:2

John's confession startled Anneza; she'd always seen him as a good Christian man. In the days, weeks and months to come she watched her husband change, drastically. She finally had to agree: his estimation of himself was correct. John had been a hard-working, kind, honorable and very religious Armenian man. But now he hungered passionately *to know Jesus* and to know the Bible for himself. He changed daily, from the inside out—not from increased effort but as if he truly were inhabited by a *different Spirit.*

In addition to John's new prayer-time and reading of the scriptures, he soon enrolled in nightly Bible classes and began actively serving others in the community and through the church. With the current condition of the economy, many people who went to church could no longer tithe to support ministry. Therefore, preachers were being paid very little or not at all. As business-owners, the Arakelians were able to share food and other items with the pastor's family and with other families. Despite an ever-worsening economy and countless uncertainties in their own lives, John's confidence and peace now seemed unshakable. "Our God hears our prayers; He's able, faithful and immutably good!" John would say. Within time, John was speaking boldly about the love of Christ to the people he met.

As Agayne and Parease grew to become lovely young girls, John and Anneza wished to have more children. John especially longed for a son of his own. Meanwhile, Anneza continued to write letters back and forth with her sister Serapi, who was nearly a young woman now. Anneza was thankful that her children were safe in America, despite the hard times, but her sister was still in danger.

Although the atmosphere and social life of Turkey had seen many reforms, news reports claimed that tens of thousands of Kurds were being slaughtered by the Turkish military. Likewise, in the Soviet Union, tens of thousands of Armenians were being executed and deported. Extreme unrest and turmoil had plagued Europe since the end of the Great War. While Europe struggled to recover from war, the Depression hit; poverty and hunger, worse than before, afflicted countries across the world. Because Europeans blamed their new (post-war) governments and leaders for their suffering, they were easily influenced by persuasive, revolutionary leaders who promised economic stability and military power. In the Soviet Union, after the Bolshevik Revolution, Vladimir Lenin had risen to power. After Lenin died, in 1924, Joseph Stalin seized power. Stalin killed political rivals and murdered millions of his own people, any he deemed as threats to his goals. Meanwhile, in Italy, Benito Mussolini rose to power, promising to restore the glory of the old Roman Empire. A former teacher and newspaper editor, Mussolini formed his own political party, the Fascist Party. Its members supported a form of totalitarian government that required extreme devotion to the nation; Mussolini eventually became the dictator. In nearby Germany, the people also blamed their financial troubles on their new government. Naturally the Germans longed for someone to stabilize their economy, and they found that someone when a skillful politician and organizer, named Adolph Hitler, promised a solution to their struggles. Hitler became popular, even in America, through his strong nationalism, stirring speeches and promises to restore Germany. As leader of the strongest political power in Germany, in 1933 he took power and subsequently outlawed all political parties except the Nazis.

Scarcely a day went by that Anneza did not feel the need to stop and pray for the continued safety of her siblings and especially for Serapi. Then one bright day, Anneza overheard of a program that could change her baby sister's life. She was overjoyed; she couldn't wait to share the news with John!

But when he arrived home that evening, John had a life-changing announcement of his own. "My dear," he said, sitting and motioning for her to sit with him, "I have something of great import to tell you."

Anneza could not help but feel apprehension. They were living in uncertain times; her mind filled with many possibilities, all of them frightening. She sat in a small chair across from her husband and mentally braced herself.

John hesitated, as if considering how to phrase his words. At last, he smiled, sighed and said, "I believe the Lord is calling me to become a preacher." When Anneza merely stared at him, speechless, John continued, "Anneza, please don't fret. I'm certain the Lord will provide for us — and we don't need all of this," he said, with a wave of his arm. "The Lord owns the cattle on a thousand hills. Besides, I've learned that to conquer one's self is to conquer life; true greatness comes from giving, not getting."

After her own moment of hesitation, Anneza smiled and nodded at her husband. "John, I will support your decision," she said, sounding braver than she felt. If ever there was a terrible time to ask what she planned to ask, this was it. With a minister for a husband, Anneza would have very little to share. However, she continued anyway, "I also have something of great import to ask you," she said. "John, will you sponsor my sister so she can come to America? And may she live with us when she arrives?"

Some months later, Anneza stood at the pier waiting patiently for her sister's ship. Anneza had never given up hope of seeing Serapi. Now, after so many years, her dream was about to come true. Standing beside Anneza, John, Agayne and Parease also scanned the crowd — trying to spot someone they had never seen before. At last the moment came; as Serapi stepped away from the dock, the whole family recognized her immediately.

"Mother," Agayne said in astonishment, "she looks like you!"

Dropping her husband's hand, Anneza began to run through the crowd toward her very lost and bewildered looking little sister. Waving her hand wildly above her head, Anneza shouted out a greeting, "Hoshgelden, Sera!! Hoshgelden!! Hoshgelden!!" Serapi, seeing her, also began to run and all but jumped into her sister's outstretched arms. "God has answered our prayers Sera!" Anneza said in Armenian, her voice cracking slightly.

After many hugs and much joyful weeping, the sisters turned and hurried back to Anneza's family, who now stood watching—with their mouths hanging open at their shy, quiet mother's sudden outburst. As she was introduced, Serapi smiled brightly at Anneza's husband and wide-eyed children. In Armenian, Serapi proclaimed, "Vai, inch sirun balikner unes du!"

"Yes, they are beautiful," Anneza replied, glancing at her children. Turning back to Serapi, Anneza continued, "and so are you, Sera! By God's hand, you're wonderfully beautiful—and it's no longer a curse!"

Just then John placed his hand on each of their shoulders. "Ladies," he said, "it's time to go home."

Page from an antique Armenian Bible

twenty-six

John

"I call heaven and earth to record this day against you, that I have set before you life and death, blessing and cursing: therefore choose life, that both thou and thy seed may live . . ."
Deuteronomy 30:19

As John's little family in America grew, he felt his joy multiply. Often he marveled at how his heart, which had grieved so long the loss of his parents and siblings, was now being filled with the love of new family members.

After the arrival of his wife's sister, their home life gradually took on a new routine; in the evenings, when Anneza would usually play her lyre for the family, she now also began teaching Sera to speak English, with the help of the children. In turn, Sera developed a habit of reading to the girls from a treasured Bible that Anneza had given her when she was a young girl. It was written in Armeno-Turkish, which was the Turkish language in the Armenian alphabet. Inside rested silk bookmarks with Bible verses. In addition, Sera was very helpful with the children, with cooking and with other chores.

Amidst all of the changes, including those of his heart and faith, John made a discovery one day that stunned him:

his lovely, quiet wife was a strong, intelligent woman of deep integrity and compassion. As a young man he'd been captured by her beauty and sweetness; now he was in awe of her complexity and rich personality. He thanked God for His marvelous plans; they always exceeded John's own limited imagination.

However, while John and his family enjoyed safety and blessings in America, their relatives in other countries endured very uncertain times. Although boxing matches were the main reason most Americans wanted radios, John bought the family a radio so they could listen to news reports. During the 1930s, several nations had taken aggressive steps that alarmed the rest of the world; in 1931 Japan seized parts of China; in 1935 Italy invaded Africa; in 1936, (ignoring the treaty of Versailles), Hitler rebuilt the German military and then stationed troops in the Rhineland, a region that had once been part of France. Then, in 1938, Germany took over its neighbor, Austria, and threatened to invade Czechoslovakia as well. Alarmed, Britain and France attempted appeasement by granting Germany the Sudetenland, a part of Czechoslovakia. Hitler accepted the gift, promising to seize no more countries. Six months later he broke his word and took over the rest of Czechoslovakia.

Anticipating another world war, several countries signed treaties and agreements during 1939. The United States was intent upon staying out of war; many Americans thought they should have stayed out of the Great War, in 1917. America was still struggling to climb out of the Great Depression, therefore, between 1935 and 1937, Congress passed three Neutrality Acts, designed to keep America neutral in any future wars.

In January of 1939, Americans responded to a poll that read: "It has been proposed to bring to this country 10,000 refugee children from Germany—most of them Jewish—to be taken care of in American homes. Should the government permit these children to come in?" Two-thirds of Americans said, "No." Not only did they want to stay out of war, they did not want Europe's refugees. The children were turned away. Later that year, in June, a ship filled with Jewish refugee families fled Germany seeking refuge in Cuba, the United States and Canada. As they begged for asylum, each country turned them away. With nowhere else to go, they turned around and sailed back to Europe.

The fact that Jewish children and families were unwanted didn't surprise most Americans. In American society, Jews were viewed as harbingers of dangerous ideologies, particularly communism and anarchism. Most Americans feared that subversive groups and spies would infiltrate the country through the tide of refugees fleeing fascist Europe. America's leaders, however, could not ignore the unsettling events in Europe as Hitler's armies swept across the continent. Eventually, appeals for help from Britain and France caused amendments to the Neutrality Acts; the United States began supplying war materials to the Allies (primarily Great Britain, France and the Soviet Union) to help them defeat Hitler and the Axis powers. Still, Americans were adamant: they wanted no further involvement with this war nor with its victims.

As John listened to his countrymen express fear of the Jews and claims that they might be working as agents for Germany, he was heartbroken. He knew how desperate a refugee's life was. He was sure the asylum seekers hadn't wanted to abandon their homes. If not for the kindness of strangers toward refugees, John would not have survived. Nevertheless, his adoptive country continued to ignore new sojourners who begged her to heed the inscription on her Statue of Liberty.

Then, on September 1st, 1939, Germany invaded Poland. In an order to his Wehrmacht commanders, on August 22, 1939—a week earlier, Adolf Hitler said, "Our strength consists in our speed and our brutality. Genghis Khan led millions of women and children to slaughter—with premeditation and a happy heart. History sees in him solely the founder of a state. It's a matter of indifference to me what a weak Western European civilization will say about me. I have issued the command—and I'll have anybody who utters but one word of criticism executed by a firing squad—that our war aim does not consist in reaching certain lines, but in the physical destruction of the enemy. Accordingly, I have placed my death-head formation in readiness—for the present only in the East—with orders to them to send to death mercilessly and without compassion, men, women, and children of Polish derivation and language. Only thus shall we gain the living space which we need. Who, after all, speaks today of the annihilation of the Armenians?"

Hitler, like most deceivers, was partially correct. But while the majority had moved on, forgetting the genocide of John's people, the Arakelians and other surviving Armenians had not. Some Jewish voices also continued to cry out, reminding the world; Henry Morgenthau, former Ambassador to Turkey, had implored the U.S. government to intercede and stop the Turkish "campaign of race extermination" against the Armenians. Later, after he lost his job because of his outspokenness, he wrote his memoir, *Ambassador Morgenthau's Story*, which contained the first full narrative about the Armenian genocide in English. Then in 1934, Franz Werfel, an Austrian Jewish novelist who escaped Hitler's death list by a hair, wrote the first major novel about the Armenian genocide, *The Forty Days of Musa Dagh*. He depicted Armenian resistance to the massacre in a small mountain village and also embedded warnings to the Jews of Europe about what would happen to them soon. The Nazis banned and burned Werfel's book in 1934.

Now, despite promises to the American public that said, "Your boys are not going to be sent into any foreign war," the leaders of the United States eventually saw a very real likelihood that Hitler would gain control of the British navy—if he wasn't stopped. Never before had America drafted young men into the armed forces before declaring war, but now they did.

Then, in 1940, Japan signed a pact with Germany and Italy, forming the Rome-Berlin-Tokyo Axis. Japan's military leaders theorized that if the American fleet at Pearl Harbor were destroyed, the United States Navy and the American people would be unable and unwilling to fight a lengthy war in the Pacific, and the United States would eventually agree to a truce with Japan. And so, early on Sunday morning, December 7th, 1941, Japanese planes, armed with bombs and torpedoes, descended upon American battleships lying at anchor in Pearl Harbor, on the Hawaiian island of Oahu. Catching the military base off-guard, the attackers destroyed twenty-one ships and over three hundred planes. Twenty-four hundred Americans died and over eleven hundred more were wounded. United States Congress responded by declaring war on Japan; Germany and Italy responded by declaring war on the United States. Thus America entered the war they had vowed to avoid.

As factories and farms in the United States hurried to provide supplies and food for American and European Allied armies, unemployment, and the Great Depression, ended almost overnight. The war had drastic effects on American life and upon the Arakelian family — all Americans were expected to become involved in the war-effort. Anneza, Sera and the girls planted a victory-garden and began rationing their own supplies. Then, when young men headed overseas on ships and planes and large numbers of women were needed to replace them on the home front, Sera took employment working at the RCA factory. When gasoline began to be rationed, John tried to manage his travels wisely. As often as he could, John drove the children across the Benjamin Franklin Bridge (which had a neon advertisement reading *No Ferry Rides*) to buy fresh meats, fruits and vegetables at the open markets of Philadelphia. The children always enjoyed going along with their father and, when they arrived home, they particularly enjoyed going to the Soda Fountain across the street.

Despite the war, Christmas came early in 1943 when a new bundle of joy was added to the Arakelian family. John and Anneza rejoiced at the arrival of their only son. They proudly called him John, the same as his father's middle name. As a toddler, little John was a cheerful boy, spending hours at play and having fun with his older siblings. His sisters enjoyed fussing over him, and Agayne especially liked to dress him in a miniature sailor outfit. Laughter filled the home whenever John, like a serious sailor, stopped his child-play to salute his family.

It wasn't until January, 1944, that United States President Franklin D. Roosevelt, under pressure from his own officials and an American Jewish community (at that time fully aware of the extent of mass murder), took action to rescue European Jews. Then, in 1945, the Second World War finally ended. It had been the deadliest military conflict in history; over sixty million people had been killed.

In 1946, the year after the war ended, little John turned three years old, and his father was asked to pastor a church in Detroit, Michigan. The war was over, peace was being restored once again and, in America, things were looking up. But while the Arakelians were making plans to move, John noticed that his wife had become increasingly tired.

twenty-seven

"As for me, I will behold thy face in righteousness: I shall be satisfied, when I awake, with thy likeness." Psalms 17:15

In the words of John's contemporary, the preacher A.W. Tozer, the close of World War II saw a radical change in the religious mood across America. In a complete reversal, religion in America suddenly became intellectually respectable. People stopped being ashamed to admit that they believed in God; society and the church shook hands and became friends. But, of course, this was not healthy. The church discovered that she could use a good many of the world's ideas, and the world found that religion was a useful technique for achieving desired ends. The *ox and the ass*, as well as the *lion and the lamb*, romped together as they had not done since Luther nailed his theses on the door of the church at Wittenberg and launched the Reformation. It was during these years that John found Gospel outreach to his own people to be especially difficult. Many Armenians already saw themselves as Christians; it was a challenge to help them see Christianity as a living faith, not just a cultural tradition. Few had any idea about being *born again,* or even about eternal life. His people knew how to endure, but they often forgot that God was the one who had rescued them.

Meanwhile, John had troubles at home as well. Anneza's tiredness seemed to increase daily; she could no longer keep up with her three-year-old son, so Sera quit her job to stay home and help. The Arakelians temporarily postponed their move while they began visiting doctors, hoping and praying for an answer that would help Anneza regain her strength.

Agayne was now eighteen, and Parease had just celebrated her thirteenth birthday. When the girls weren't busy with their studies, they pitched in to help more as well; they were both old enough to understand that something was terribly wrong.

When medical tests finally confirmed Anneza's diagnosis, the news was not at all what they had hoped for.

"Your wife is in the advanced stages of breast cancer," the doctor said.

Despite his deep faith in God's goodness, John was devastated. How could this happen to the woman he planned to share his entire life with? The mother of his precious children?

In the days and weeks that followed, John dropped his face to his hands repeatedly and prayed, "Please Lord save my dear wife! Please let this cup pass!" John was willing to give everything to find a cure, and Anneza was willing to undergo whatever treatments were necessary. But still, despite good doctors and many prayers, she grew worse.

One rainy night, John sat beside her bed praying, thinking and making plans for what they might try next. The dark hours of the night marched by slowly, measured only by the drumming of the rain on the roof and his wife's restlessness and labored breathing.

When he noticed that she was awake again, he patted her hand very gently to remind her that he was nearby.

"John," she said weakly, "won't you go away and get some sleep?"

Smiling very wearily, he replied, "I'm not one bit tired."

In the dim glow of the night light, he watched her slowly return his smile. "You should rest, John," she said.

Though he dared not tell her, he was frightened by how pale she'd become in the past few days. But he believed in miracles . . . And she was still telling him what to do. That gave him hope.

"God knows you're a hard worker, John," she said, "and you're capable; you do a great many things and you do them well. But you can't protect me from this. Stop worrying and go to bed."

"I will not quit," he replied. "We'll try new doctors! And when you're well again, we'll go on vacation; I'll take you anywhere you want to go."

"You can't go where I'm going," she responded. "You'll come later, but you cannot come now."

"Anneza, God can heal you," he said, choking back the emotions that he felt. "Look at all He's done in the past. He's never forsaken us before; He will not forsake us now."

"He will not forsake me," Anneza agreed, now speaking in their native language. "But you will lose me soon, Armen John Arakelian."

John shook his head. "I'm not letting you go," he replied in Armenian.

Anneza sighed slowly. "Regardless," she said, "you will lose me soon."

John continued to shake his head slowly back and forth as a tear escaped his eye and wet his cheek. Although the cancer had abused her physically, he marveled at the beauty of his wife. He watched in thick silence as she drew in slow, shallow breaths; he no longer heard the rain.

"Tell me again . . . about your mother," she asked, when the silence had grown too long. "I don't want to abandon my children . . . but like your mother, where is my choice?"

"Your body has weakened, Anneza," John replied. "Only your body, Love. Likewise, my mother's devotion to us was endless," he replied. "It didn't dim when she was gone—because her love was not simply her own.

"It took me many years to learn this, Anneza, but my mother's light and love were His light and His love, shining through her as she trusted Him. He cared for me; He protected me; He sustained me—first through my mother, then through others when He took her into His presence."

"I long to meet her," Anneza replied. She paused, out of breath but looking like she had more to say.

John placed his hand on her pale forehead and stroked softly across her brow.

At last she continued, "You know, John, people say that God could have saved the Armenians. They say God didn't care enough about them, or about your mother to save her . . . But they're wrong. I'm convinced your mother heard the words, *Well done, good and faithful servant,* when she left you and stood before His throne."

"Anneza," John replied, "do you remember where Jesus is? What does the Bible tell us?"

Taking a long, slow breath, she answered, "After rising from the grave, He ascended to Heaven. He sits at the right hand of the Father."

"Yes," John answered with a smile, "you're correct. It was not to an angel that God said, 'Sit at my right hand until I make your enemies a footstool for your feet'—but it was to His son, who is the exact likeness of the Father. The

Son, whom now waits to receive His bride—the church—we who are *His* and who are sealed with the Holy Spirit.

"But, Anneza, do you remember, in the book of Acts, when the martyr Stephen was dying? Stephen looked up and saw Heaven open. He saw the Father and the Son. Where was Jesus then, when Stephen was dying?" he asked.

"Jesus was standing," Anneza replied; a soft smile brightened her face. "He stood up at the right hand of the Father," she said.

John nodded in agreement. "Precious in the sight of the Lord is the death of his saints," he quoted.

"Thank you," she answered. Then, with a determined tone, she added, "John, I have a request. Please don't deny me."

"Never, my dear," he replied. "I am at your disposal—ask and it's yours."

To this Anneza shook her head slowly. "You answer too quickly. I want you to think seriously about the future, for just a moment."

"I'm seriously thinking I will love you forever, Anneza. That's in the future," he said.

"Very well," she replied. "This is my request: please don't let the children lose Sera, when they lose me."

Stunned, John answered immediately, "Of course not. I would never separate the children from your sister, Anneza. They love her, and she them."

"John, you're not yet an old man. You're handsome and good . . . when you're a widower—"

"Please, Anneza," he interrupted, "our God is the healer; I haven't given up my plans to spend the rest of my life with you."

But she continued, "Many women will wish to marry you. They may love you, but will they love my children as I do? Will they love my children even as Sera does? Especially little John—he's spent more time in Sera's arms than in my own."

"Anneza," he said, "the future is in God's hands. Nothing is impossible for Him."

"John, Sera is a beautiful young woman. You are a minister—a man of God. When I'm gone, you cannot allow her to remain in your home. It would look scandalous."

"Well, yes. It would," he said at last. "I . . . "

John was speechless.

Anneza nodded. "She'll be forced to leave; the children will lose her, just as they've lost me. Oh, she'll still be around, but she will eventually marry. Her husband may or may not let her continue to be involved in the care of our children . . . John, this cancer will take both Sera and I away from the children. It will."

John stared at her, realization dawning.

"There is only one way to stop this disease from robbing our children twice," she said. "They need her, John. And she needs them. She will make an excellent mother . . . and an excellent wife."

Heavy silence filled the room once more. It occurred to John that the sun had risen; its first rays were coming through the cracks between the blinds and dancing off the sheets at Anneza's shoulders. He didn't blame her for asking, but her question ripped at his heart, stealing his carefully-guarded joy, deducting from the quickly-fading gift of being in her presence . . . Priceless minutes ticked by before he could speak again. "Anneza, have you mentioned this to Sera?" he asked at last.

Anneza smiled and closed her eyes.

Moving his palm from her forehead, he reached for her hand and held it gently. "I agree to pray about it, Anneza," he said. "I will pray and consider. But please, let's talk of other things now."

With a faint shrug of her graceful shoulders, she responded quietly, "If you honor my desire, even when I'm gone, then I'll believe you love me forever." Then, with a weak squeeze to his hand, she changed the subject.

"Tell me, Pastor . . . what do you think it will be like to enter into God's presence? Is there a chance I'll hear, *Well done, good and faithful servant*? I believe . . . I believe that believing is what He requires. And I do believe Jesus is the Son of God; He died a ransom for my sins; He rose again . . . I believe He is the only way to the Father . . . but, John, God knows me. He knows my fear. He knows I have doubted . . . at times. I've asked for forgiveness, and He is faithful to forgive . . . . but He is so perfect . . ." she paused and searched for words. At last, in a whisper that was barely audible, she concluded, "He's terrifyingly perfect."

"My dear," John responded, "I cannot speak for God. However, it would not surprise me one bit if you hear a voice, like thunder and many waters, shouting out, "Hoshgelden! Hoshgelden! Hoshgelden, my bride! Enter into the joy of the Lord!"

Just then, John noticed that she was sleeping again. His eyes lingered long upon her face, now bathed in radiant morning sunshine. Placing a kiss on her cheek, he whispered, "I will love you forever, Anneza."

twenty-eight

"Seek ye the Lord while he may be found, call ye upon him while he is near: Let the wicked forsake his way, and the unrighteous man his thoughts: and let him return unto the Lord, and he will have mercy upon him; and to our God, for he will abundantly pardon." Isaiah 55:6-7

Anneza's death was devastating for the Arakelian family. But for the sake of the children, and his wife's wishes, John married Sera privately as soon as the timing was appropriate. Despite their great loss, they both believed the marriage to be God's will; the children agreed and were greatly relieved and comforted by Sera's continued love and care. After a short time, the family moved to Detroit to begin John's pastorate of a small church. There, out of necessity, John re-established his cleaning and tailoring business.

During the years following the Second World War, despite widespread fears of communism (which was expanding worldwide), America enjoyed a time of calm. Church attendance soared from fifty million churchgoing Americans in 1940, to eighty million in the late 1950s. For many families it was an era of comfort and prosperity. The Arakelians also enjoyed a season of blessings, and after two years serving the little church in Detroit, John and Sera had their first child. They named her Roseann. Her older sisters, and brother John, were delighted; God had increased their family again, thereby increasing their joy.

Like her older siblings, Roseann was a delightful and beautiful child. However, Roseann had great difficulty breathing. When she was diagnosed with asthma, the doctor recommended that the family move to the warmer, drier climate found in the west, specifically California. John and Sera sought the Lord for guidance. After many prayers, they believed the Lord was directing them to the west coast. So, in the spring of 1950, they loaded their car and left for California.

With the help of an Armenian friend, John found housing in a quiet neighborhood in Pasadena. He also re-established his cleaning and tailoring shop nearby. But his many years in the business, and the harsh dry-cleaning chemicals, had been hard on John's body, especially his hands. Seeing that he needed help, Sera became his shop assistant in addition to running their household.

The Arakelians loved California—it was a large oasis with beautiful palm trees and mountainous foothills. John particularly loved the cities of Palm Springs and Fresno; their exceptionally hot and arid climates reminded him of his homeland.

California was a hub for Armenian immigrants and their descendents. In fact, the Lord had led John and Sera to the part of America with the very largest population of Armenian-Americans. However, although John connected with the local Armenian believers, he received exceptional warmth and acceptance from non-Armenians who longed to hear his life story. Hence, he began the work of an evangelist. He preached at many venues and even became involved in radio ministry. His family was also involved in prison ministry at detention camps in the foothills of Los Angeles County.

Meanwhile, a strong breeze of change hit America. While the post-war period was known as an idyllic time of comfort, prosperity and church-growth, prosperity was for middle and upper-class *Whites* only. Minority groups and immigrants experienced only poverty and discrimination. Equality was distrusted and considered a communistic lie; racial intermingling was shameful, even in church.

Therefore, by the late 1950s, a generation of underprivileged minorities arose demanding their equal rights; although their protests began peacefully, violence resulted.

As an evangelist and preacher to immigrants and minorities, as well as Whites, John warned crowds that the civil rights movement was being exploited by militant Islamic groups who promised them prosperity but were capable of delivering only hatred, suffering and destruction. John was convinced that Americans were simply unaware that Islam had always been a religion of the sword—never one freely chosen. So he endeavored to protect the unsuspecting Americans from what he knew to be a deadly evil; he authored a booklet titled *The False Prophet of Mecca*. He implored Americans to escape the condemnation and horror of following a false prophet and to, instead, be reconciled to a loving, merciful God through the atoning blood and resurrection of Christ. If they would wake up and do this, he said, their country could continue strongly forever.

About this time, a new generation of privileged White kids grew up bitter and disillusioned by the emptiness of their prosperity and the coldness of their religious-parent's lives. This hippie-counterculture rejected the fearful, prejudiced society of their parents. They desired peace and strove to love their fellowman. Abandoning materialism, they lived communally, without rules or morals and used drugs liberally. They also sought to find meaning for their lives by exploring all spiritual beliefs. It was an era of confusion and turmoil. But by the great mercy of God, while civil and moral crisis rocked America, the country was suddenly awash in an even stronger wave—it was an irrefutable moving of the *Holy Spirit*.

Prior to 1955, mainstream religion rejected anything they considered *supernatural*. They declared that God had stopped giving men spiritual gifts after the Bible was complete; neither did He give messages or instructions to modern people. However, during the 1950s and 1960s, Pentecostal and Charismatic movements simultaneously burst to life within churches of America. When the Arakelians arrived in California, this storm of change had just begun to leap from the obscure into the mainstream—and it had all started just down the road from John and Sera's new home.

Suddenly, countless Americans testified of dramatic encounters with God; preachers suddenly understood that being filled with the Holy Spirit was the means to empowerment for Christian life and service. They taught that the supernatural events in the New Testament should be understood literally and could be expected in the life of the true believer. They saw God do miracles, such as healing the sick; they believed they received visions, promptings from God and even direct messages through the indwelling Holy Spirit.

As this new spiritual awakening refused to stay inside church-buildings, vast crowds of hippies worshipped God in tents (just miles from Armen's new home) and were baptized by the thousands in the ocean or wherever else they could find water. They changed overnight from drug-addicts into sober (and very vocal) *Jesus freaks*. They became known for unashamed racial intermingling and their deep love for one another.

While these changes were obvious during the Arakelian's first decade in California, the spiritual shift actually began forty-five years earlier, in Los Angeles, on Azusa Street — just ten miles from John's new home.

Although the revival on Azusa Street was considered by many to be over-the-top and non-biblical in some ways, it had certainly been unnatural. From its start in 1906, until 1915, countless thousands flocked to the little run-down church on Azusa Street where a one-eyed, Black preacher seldom preached a sermon. Instead he sat on a milk crate, with his head inside another crate, and prayed. Now and then he would shout out, "Repent!" Despite objections to the disorderly meetings, those who attended the revival were unquestionably changed; they carried this transformation around the world. Eventually it hit the mainstream church.

Although the Azusa Street revival received most of the notice, another event had actually caused it; between the years 1900 and 1912, a group of over two-thousand immigrants came to California from the region of Mount Ararat, in the heart of Armenia. These immigrants, known as "jumpers" for their charismatic beliefs and style of worship, refused to stop on the east coast when they arrived in America. Instead, they immediately traveled across the country and settled on the west coast of California, near Los Angeles.

Not only did the coming of the "jumpers" usher in a new spiritual age in America, but they warned that a soon-to-come Charismatic movement would be a forerunner of the Second Coming of Christ—in which He would return to judge the inhabitants of the Earth. And there would be, they said, only two classifications that mattered: those who trusted in the atoning sacrifice of Jesus Christ, and those who did not.

But first, they said, there would come a murderous persecution of Christians in America. They claimed that God would call His listening people to flee from America prior to the coming persecution. Many believers respected the warnings of these immigrants; after all, they fled their homeland during a time of peace, simply because a prophet had announced that an unspeakable tragedy was soon to come upon Armenia. Their leader was a preacher by the name of Efim Klubniken, otherwise known as the

Boy Prophet. Just two years after the last of the group followed this Russian-born preacher out of Armenia, sudden and total destruction came to every village and town they had left.

Men like Armen John Arakelian had difficulty believing that a great persecution of Christians could ever happen in America, due to her long heritage of the Christian faith. However, John didn't believe in coincidences and was convinced that God had brought him—an unlikely, lonely Armenian boy—to the shores of America for a reason. Therefore, John cried out fervently to many crowds, saying:

"Today our country is besieged with religious organizations which deny, to a greater or lesser degree, the absolute atoning power of the blood of the Lord which bought them; and our people, having left the only true God, fall into sin upon sin as their lusts lead them on! Of all such teaching God's word warns us that they bring upon themselves swift destruction.

"As we see such teachings appear in our country today; as we see Moslem mosques rising in our land, which once had the Bible for its standard," he said, "let us renew our allegiance to the Lord Jesus Christ. The captain of our salvation does not lie dead and powerless in a grave in Medina, as Mohammed does; He lives in Heaven, at the right hand of God, and He has all power!"

John continued to preach that if people would return to God, through Christ, the beautiful nation of the United

States of America could be restored and regain her former blessings and glory. But, he conceded, if Americans continued to reject Christ, and especially if they embraced the false prophet of Mecca, there would certainly come a day of incredible horror and bloodshed in America.

In his later seasons, John pastored a Native American mission church in the Downey/South Gate area. One chilly Sunday morning, he and Sera exited their house and walked hand-in-hand to their parked car. The years of pressing clothes and dry-cleaning had left John with deteriorating arthritis in his hands. Nevertheless, he always opened doors for Sera, as a matter of respect and gentlemanly manners.

This morning however, John's hands cooperated even less than usual. Sera waited patiently as he dropped the keys three times, then struggled to unlock her door and finally to work the handle. At last he had her securely inside the vehicle; he then repeated the difficult and lengthy process to get himself inside and seated in the driver's seat. After finally inserting the key into the ignition and turning the engine on, putting the vehicle into gear proved too difficult. After many unsuccessful tries, he turned the engine off, laid his twisted hands in his lap and dropped his head.

"I'm sorry, Dear," he said. "It seems my old body no longer possesses the strength to do the Lord's work."

They sat there, silent for a time. At last John raised his head and sighed. "Then I said, I will not make mention of

Him, nor speak any more in His name. But His word was in mine heart as a burning fire shut up in my bones, and I was weary with forbearing, and I could not stay," he quoted.

Without a word, Sera got out of the car, walked around to John's side and smoothly opened his door. "Move over," she said with a grin. "Let's go set the world on fire."

"And the devil that deceived them
was cast into the lake of fire and brimstone,
where the beast and false prophet are,
and shall be tormented day and night
for ever and ever."

Revelation 20:10

BLACK SEA

EASTERN TURKEY

MEDITERRANEAN SEA

ISTANBUL

ADAPAZARI

ESKISEHIR

ANKARA

KONYA

NEVSEHIR

NIGDE

ADANA

MERSIN

URFA

ALLEPO

DAYR AZOR
(MASSACRE SPOT)

GOING TO MASSACRE
RETURN TO FREEDOM

Copyright 1970
by Armen John Arakelian

The False Prophet

by Armen John Arakelian, 1966

We read in God's word, *"There is one God, and one mediator between God and men, the man Christ Jesus."* (1 Timothy 2:5)

If this is true, indeed, then all men must turn to this man, Christ Jesus, to have peace between themselves and the one true God. With Him we can say, truly, *"I can do all things through Christ which strengtheneth me." "Without Him we are, "wretched, and miserable, and poor, and blind, and naked."* (Philippians 4:13, Revelation 3:17).

If we believe God's testimony concerning Himself and His Son, Jesus, we are forced to conclude that any other person who attempts to stand in the gap between God and men is a pretender, and a deceiver of men.

Now let us consider, for a moment, the claims of Mohammed. Seven hundred million people *(in 1966)* bow five times a day toward the city of Mecca, reaffirming aloud their belief that, "There is no god but Allah, and Mohammed is his prophet." They follow the system of religion set up by the man Mohammed nearly fourteen hundred years ago. They pray to Allah and serve him with alms giving and fasting and pilgrimages. Their devotion is to Allah, and they follow their guidebook, *The Koran*, given to them by their prophet, Mohammed.

Islam, meaning submission to God, is the name given this religion by its founder, Mohammed. Its the name preferred by its adherents as well. In practice, this submission degenerates into mere fatalism, or acceptance of circumstances.

This man Mohammed did establish a form of worship, but was he actually a messenger sent by the one true God to reveal Himself to men? Remembering the perfect life and atoning death, and powerful resurrection, of the Lord Jesus—to say nothing of the miracles he wrought—we can see in His [Jesus'] life God incarnate manifested. We can ask, in all fairness, *what about the man Mohammed?*

As we look at his [Mohammed's] life, we search in vain for a manifestation of the glory of God. We see a man, from among the Arabs of the desert, who preached that his countrymen should turn from the idols they worshipped and worship Allah, who was (according to Mohammed) the God of Abraham. However, aside from realizing that God could not be worshipped in the form of idols, Mohammed was lacking in knowledge of the one true God—the Jews of his time rejected his claim to the title of a prophet because he was not even well versed in the Old Testament.

In time, as Mohammed's teaching was ignored, tolerated, or rejected by the majority of his countrymen, and his following was minor, Mohammed made a decision—he would not wait for men to accept him. His action is aptly described by a twentieth century Mohammedan biographer, Essad Bey (in his book *Mohammed*): "The world did not wish to come to Mohammed of its own accord and so it was that he decided to use force." "The messenger of God took many a sin upon himself, he spilled blood, ruled brutally and heartlessly, dealt craftily and slyly." "From now on it was to be the sword and not the word which was to decide the fate of their faith."[1]

Mohammed did not offer a religion to be freely accepted or rejected by those to whom he preached; he spread his religion with the sword in the traditional Arabian style of war and pillage. He gave his approval to the pagan customs of Arabia: pilgrimages to Mecca, worship of the black rock of Mecca, and polygamy. He sanctioned them by his own practice of them. He demonstrated a genius for leadership in organizing the Arab tribes into a single force with the common bond of his religion.

However, the "prophet of God", as he called himself, led a life of immorality by any standards, even those he set up in his Koran, which falls far short of the standards of a holy God revealed in His word, the Bible.

Mohammed's faith in the power of his own system of religion was such that he could say only, "If the mountain will not come to Mohammed, then Mohammed will go to the mountain." The record of his followers through the ages is a history of murder, massacre, pillage, hate—all that man, left to follow his own desires, can devise.

In her book *Non-Christian Religions*, Ione Lowman, of the Bible Institute of Los Angeles, has an excellent short study of the tenets of Mohammedanism. The following excerpt from her book will serve to inform us of the beliefs and practices of this religion. [2]

Who then was Mohammed? Born in 570 A. D. in Mecca, Mohammed lost his parents very early in life and was brought up in the main by his grandfather and an uncle. The grandfather was a leader in the powerful Koreish clan, and no doubt instilled in the boy Mohammed some ideas of superiority and some principles of leadership. At the age of 25 Mohammed married Khadijah, a wealthy widow, in whose employ he had been a caravan trader. At the age of 40 he received his first "revelation," supposedly through the angel Gabriel in person. This was his call to become a prophet, his commission being to decry the vices and idolatry of his fellow citizens, and to proclaim a coming judgment. It is difficult to determine his motives throughout most of his career, but it would appear that he was perfectly sincere in this first purpose. It is said that Mohammed's actions at times showed that probably he suffered from some mental disease, of intermittent character, which doubtless was responsible for many of his "revelations."

His wife was a great source of encouragement to him in this new mission, and the successful start that the Prophet made can be accredited largely to her influence. Not that the new faith was received well in Mecca. At first there were gathered around him only a little handful of converts; but they were sincere in their worship of the "one true God," and were willing to endure persecution in following the doctrines of their leader. This was encouraging to Mohammed, and he preached with more boldness, the result being that persecution became so acute he was compelled to flee to Medina, where he already had a group of believers.

This flight, or "Hegira," in the year 622, marks the beginning of the Moslem era, from which the Moslem computes his dates. In Medina, Mohammed became a political, as well as religious, leader, assuming virtually the dictatorship of the city. It was from Medina that Islam began to be propagated by the sword. Mohammed sent expeditions first against the Jews, then as his power grew, against others. In the eighth year of the Hegira, he entered his own native city with 10,000 men, and taking it without a battle, destroyed all the idols in the Kaaba and made the people take an oath of allegiance to him.

As to his moral character, there seems to have come a great change with the death of his wife, Khadiha, for he married two other women within the year following. Before the end of his life he took eleven wives and two concubines, thus not only breaking his own precept as written in the Koran, but also breaking the old pagan Arabian law. It is stated that his relations with women are unfit for print. It is also known that his nature was vindictive, seeking revenge even to the extent of murder. Some writers would defend the Prophets character, but our estimate is taken from the records of his life as written down by his own devoted adherents.

These records are all we have of his life, and they condemn him. This is Islam's founder and leader—the ideal, the example of the Moslem world. His life and character give the keynote to the character and practices of Islam down through the centuries.

MOSLEM IMMAN and DIN

All investigators divide the religion of Islam into two parts, entitled the Immam, or articles of faith, and the Din, or practice of faith.

There are six main articles to the Immam: God, Angels, Books, Prophets, Day of Judgment, and Predestination. (These six articles are very clearly stated and explained by Dr. Robert E. Hume in his book The World's Living Religions.)

"The Essential Mohammedan Beliefs:

Any intelligent Moslem can state with ease and definiteness his six main beliefs, as formulated in traditional theology.

(1) Belief in the One God, Allah.
The first and foremost item in Islam is monotheism. This is taught repeatedly in the Koran, and forms the first half of the Moslem creed.
(2) Belief in Angels.
They intercede with Allah for the forgiveness of men. Eight angels support the throne of Allah. Nineteen angels guard hell. Gabriel is the archangel. He is [erroneously] called the "Holy Spirit." Jinn, genii, are a group of spirits midway between men and angels; they are both good and evil. Some of them have "submitted themselves," and thereby have become Moslems. One of the jinn is the devil. He is designated in the Koran as "shaitin," from the Hebrew "Satan," also as "Iblis," from the Greek "Diablos." This tempter is a very important personage in the Koran. His is accompanied

by a group of especially rebellious spirits, "Shaiyatin," devils.

(3)   Belief in the Koran.

Allah has sent down various books, among them the Hebrew Torah; and   lastly the Koran to Mohammed.

(4)   Belief in the Prophets of Allah.

Twenty-eight such are named in the Koran. Twenty-two of them are from the Old Testament, including Adam, Enoch, Methuselah, Noah, Abraham, Lot, Ishmael, Isaac, Jacob, Moses, David, Solomon, Elijah, Elisha, and Jonah. There are three from the New Testament-Zacharias, John the Baptist, and Jesus. Among the Mohammedan prophets outside the Bible is Alexander the Great. Mohammed is the last and greatest of all the preceding prophets.

(5)   Belief in Judgment, Paradise, and Hell.

At the end of the world there will be a resurrection of all the dead on "the day of coming forth." The great judgment day of Allah and the unity of God are the two messages of Mohammed from the beginning to the end of his preaching. The two earliest of the revelations, as now classified in a chronological order of the preachments of Mohammed, contain this message of the judgment day to come. Mohammed, like some of the Hebrew prophets, delivered thunderous warnings of doomsday impending with decisive rewards and punishments. Concrete pictures are presented of the balance scales, which will be used to weight the good and evil deeds of each soul, even to the weight of a grain of mustard seed. Paradise, with abundant pleasures for the senses, is pictured awaiting the pious believers in Allah. More than a score of passages, almost without exception, refer to gardens and flowing rivers, luxurious food and ease, and varied sensuous pleasures. Hell for

the wicked unbelievers is presented repeatedly
with vivid, gruesome pictures.
        6)   Belief in the Divine Decrees.
        Everything is predestined by Allah's ap-
pointment, even men's belief and unbelief. [3]

The preeminent doctrine obviously is monotheism, yet it
is not the monotheism of either Judaism or Christianity.
The attributes of God are unity, omnipotence, and mercy.
This last, however, is in theory only, for the God of Islam
is unreasonable and full of caprice [impulse, whims, silly
thoughts]. Zwemer says, "absolute sovereignty and ruthless omnipotence are his chief attributes while the Christian truth that God is Love is to the learned Moslem
blasphemy and, to the ignorant, an enigma." [4]

Their idea of God is one who threatens awful punishments, and who is standing off, only watching for the
judgment day when he can wreak vengeance on the poor,
helpless creatures of earth. There is absolutely no thought
of Fatherhood. Islam is called the "worse form of monotheism." As a result of this [false] conception of God, Islam has, according to Clarke, "Hardened into despotism,
stiffened into formalism, and sunk into death."

What a true and concise description these words give of
this religion! I doubt that even a Mohammedan who has
definite hope of heaven looks forward to it with any great
amount of joy, for their ideals are low, and they know
nothing of the joy of a redeemed soul.

Consider this comparison of the concept of God as found
in each of the three universal [monotheistic] faiths:

Mohammed teaches God above us.

Moses teaches God above us and, yet, with us.

Jesus Christ teaches God above us, God with us, and God within us.

The transcendent god of Mohammedanism will not suffice; the immanent god of the Hindu does not satisfy our needs; we must have the God who is revealed in the person of Jesus Christ—none other is adequate for the longings of the human soul, and none other is able to give the peace of sins forgiven, and the joy of new life, as we have in Him.

There is a definite relation between the Immam, or belief, and the Din, or practice. All who believe and confess the Creed and Moslems and upon them is laid the commandment to fulfill definite duties. These duties, the Din, are five in number, and have been called the "pillars of the religion."

First, is the repetition of the Creed, publicly and privately, "Allah is one God and Mohammed is his prophet," or as translated by Zwemer, "There is no god but God; Mohammed is the apostle of God." Someone has called this short creed the watchword [password] of Islam. It is repeated in Arabic every day, on all occasions. Note that many followers are not Arabs and have no understanding of Arabic. But the creed is not recited in any other language than the original Arabic.

Next in importance is the practice of prayer, enjoined by the Koran and considered a duty by every true Moslem. There are set times for prayer: dawn, noon, before sunset, sunset, and after sunset. Direction also is important; the devotee must face Mecca. "The words used during this exercise consist of Koran phrases, and short chapters, which include praise, confession and prayer for guidance. Personal, private petitions are allowed after the liturgical prayers, but they are not common." [4]

The third "pillar" is the giving of alms, a meritorious act and especially commanded by the Koran.

Fasting, the fourth "pillar" is traditional and is a means of gaining merit or rewards. All good acts are supposed to lead to rewards but fasting leads to the greatest number.

The special fast of Mohammedanism is known as the fast of Ramadan. "O believers, a fast is prescribed for you . . . the month of Ramadan shall ye fast ------ eat and drink, until you can plainly distinguish a white thread from a black thread by daylight: then keep the fast until the night . . ." [5]

The pious Moslem takes nothing into his body, not so much as a drop of water, from sunrise to sunset. This entails little hardship for the man of wealth. He may take his ease in cool seclusion. How about the man who must labor under the pitiless desert sun during the long summer day without one sip of the water God has so graciously supplied for the needs of the body!? Surely this is a religion of works. The following quotation illustrates this point: "Prayer carries us half-way to God, fasting brings us to the door of his palace, and alms procures us admission." [6]

The pilgrimage to Mecca, the fifth "pillar" has proved one of the greatest unifying agencies of the faith. Even today pilgrims from other lands return to their homes convinced of the greatness and glory of Islam.

LIBERTY through CHRIST

At this point you may ask, "What has all this to do with me? Surely if we just forget the past and concentrate on making friends and understanding our enemies we can work out our differences and live peacefully." Let us go back for a moment and reexamine the requirement that a holy God makes upon sinful mankind.

Like all whose lives are dedicated to the Lord Jesus Christ and his Gospel (I) John Arakelian firmly believe Jesus' words, *"No man cometh to the Father but by me."* All mankind is divided by God the Father into two groups: those who obey His Gospel and accept His Son as their own Savior (for their own sins) on the one side; and those on the other side who reject God's precious gift of His Son. To the latter group but one promise is given: they will follow a path that leads from sin to sin and has but one destination: hell—without God, without hope.

"For God so loved the world, that he gave his only begotten Son, that whosoever believeth in Him should not perish, but have everlasting life. For God sent not His Son into the world to con-

demn the world; but that the world through Him might be saved. He that believeth on Him is not condemned; but he that believeth not is condemned already, because he hath not believed in the name of the only begotten Son of God." (John 3:16-18)

In years past our forefathers have placed their trust in God's only Son, leaving their homelands to find a place where they could worship God according to His word. God has truly blessed us greatly as a nation as we have sought to serve Him, witnessing to others the blessedness of serving the one true God who alone is able to save to the uttermost all those who come unto Him.

But today our country is besieged with religious organizations which deny, to a greater or lesser degree, the absolute atoning power of the blood of the Lord which bought them; and our people, having left the only true God, fall into sin upon sin as their lusts lead them on. Of all such teaching, God's word warns us that they bring upon themselves swift destruction.

As we see such teachings appear in our country today; as we see Muslim mosques rising in our land which once had the Bible for its standard; let us renew our allegiance to the Lord Jesus Christ. The captain of our salvation does not lie dead and powerless in a grave in Medina as Mohammed does; He lives in heaven at the right hand of God and He has all power.

Our first president, George Washington, said, "It is impossible to govern the world rightly without God and the Bible." Our Bible has some definite directions that we should heed. Galatians 1:7-8 warns us:

". . . but there be some that trouble you, and would pervert the gospel of Christ. But though we, or an angel from heaven, preach any other gospel unto you than that which we have preached unto you, let him be accursed."

We can be comforted and strengthened by 1 Corinthians 15:58:

"Therefore, my beloved brethren, be ye steadfast, unmovable, always abounding in the work of the Lord, forasmuch as ye know that your labor is not in vain in the Lord."

2 Corinthians 1:4 says:

"Who comforteth us in all our tribulation, that we may be able to comfort them which are in any trouble, by the comfort wherewith we ourselves are comforted of God;" and 2 Peter 3:14 says, *"Wherefore, beloved, seeing that ye look for such things, be diligent that ye may be found of him in peace, without spot, and blameless."*

Let us who live in America heed [this] warning and not forsake the faith in God which is our heritage. Our God has never forsaken us nor failed us; let us be true to Him. Let us thank God anew for the land, which He has given us, and for the freedom to worship Him according to His word. Let us "be strong, and of a good courage."

Let us remain faithful to our only Lord and Savior, Jesus Christ, proclaiming His name throughout the earth.

1. Essad Bey, "Mohammed" tr. by Helmut L. Ripperger Langmans, New York: Green and Company, 1936, pp. 177-179.

2. Lowman, Ione, Ph.D., Th.D., "Non-Christian Religions" Wheaton, Illinois: Von Kompen Press, pp. 86-88, 92-96.

3. Hume, R. E., "The World's Living Religions." New York: Scribner's, 1929, p 225.

4. Zwemer, S. M., "The Moslem World", New York: Eaton, 1908, p. 60, 71.

5. Sale, "The Koran", Chapter 1.

Glossary

Abdul Hamid 11 - The 34th Sultan of the Ottoman Empire who ruled from September, 1842 to February, 1918. He received the nickname, "Red Sultan" because approximately three-hundred thousand Armenians were brutally slaughtered during his reign.

Allied Powers - Essentially the countries of France, Britain and Russia made up the allied powers during WWI. Later in the war, Italy and the United States of America joined them in lending additional manpower and material to the war effort.

Ambassador - An individual who acts as a representative of his country in communicating with foreign nations.

Armistice - An armistice is the effective end of a war, when the warring parties agree to stop fighting. It is derived from the Latin arma, meaning weapons and statium, meaning a stopping.

Attaché - A person who is a civil servant.

Battle of Srikamish - A military conflict between Russia and the Ottoman Empire during WWI This event occurred between December 22, 1914 and January 17, 1915.

Bayonet - A spear.

Bedawee (Bedouin) - A nomadic tribe inhabiting the deserts of Arabia, Jordan, Syria, and parts of the Sahara.

Cappadocia - Ancient district in east-central Anatolia, on the plateau north of the Taurus Mountains, in the center of present-day Turkey. Historical boundaries have varied throughout history.

Caravan - A convoy or procession of travelers, including pack animals - especially camels, who journeyed together for safety in passing through the desert.

Cobbler - A person who mends shoes for a livelihood.

Commemorate - To honor or memorialize persons or events.

Deportation - The act of transporting an individual or groups of people out of the country; banishment.

Dowry - An ancient custom that involves the transfer of parental property at the marriage of a daughter.

Franc - The official national currency of France until the euro was adopted in 1999.

Gangplank - A movable plank used as a ramp to board or disembark from a ship or vessel.

Gethsemane - A garden near Jerusalem, Israel; here Jesus prayed (regarding his impending crucifixion), "O my Father, if it be possible, let this cup pass from me: nevertheless not as I will, but as thou wilt."

Great Depression - A term used to describe the worldwide economic collapse which occurred in the 1930s. The timing of the Great Depression varied across nations; however, in most countries it started in 1929 and lasted until the late 1930s. It was the longest, deepest, and most widespread depression of the 20th century.

Great War - The first global war, mostly centered in Europe. It began on 28 July 1914 and lasted until 11 November 1918. One of the deadliest conflicts in history, this event paved the way for major political changes, including revolutions in many of the nations involved.

Hoshgelden - 1900's greeting in Turkey, in the most common language of the land (spoken by all people-groups). It's meaning was: "You have come pleasantly," or "We welcome you!"

Infidel - In the Islamic religion, the word refers to a person who rejects or disbelieves in Allah (an Arabic term for God) or who hides, denies, or pays no attention to the beliefs held by devout Muslims.

Islam - The word means "submission." It is the religion of Muslims as set forth in the Koran and teaches there is only one God, Allah, based on the teachings of the prophet Muhammad.

Jihad - A holy war undertaken by Muslims in defense of the Islamic faith.

Kinship - Blood relationships.

Labor Camp - A detention facility where inmates are forced to work.

Lavash - A type of Armenian bread.

Lira - The name of a currency in Turkey.

Lyre - A stringed instrument similar to a harp but smaller. It was popular in ancient Greece and throughout the Middle East.

Malaria - An infectious disease caused by parasites that are carried by mosquitos and transmitted to humans.

Mallet - An appliance that was used for coffee grinding.

Mecca - A city located in western Saudi Arabia that is revered by Muslims as the birthplace of Mohammed.

Metropolis - A large city which has a significant economic, political, and cultural center for a country or region; an important hub for regional or international connections, commerce, and communications.

Missionary - A person sent by a church into an area to carry on evangelism or other activities, such as working in schools or hospitals.

Mohammed - The founder of Islam.

Mosque - A Muslim place of worship.

Mosul - A city in northern Iraq, on the Tigris River, opposite the ruins of Nineveh. It is located in the region of ancient Babylon.

Mount Ararat - A range of mountains in eastern Turkey near the borders of Armenia and Iran. It is the place where the Bible says Noah's ark came to rest.

Naturalized Citizen - The legal act or process by which a non-citizen in a country may acquire citizenship.

Nomad - A member of a community of people who live in different locations, moving from one place to another.

Oasis - A fertile area in the desert which surrounds a spring or other water source.

Pool of Bethesda - A pool in Jerusalem believed to have had healing powers; it is the place where Jesus healed a paralyzed man (John 5:2).

Red Moon - A lunar eclipse that causes the moon to appear red or copper; it is also known as a "blood moon."

Refuge - Any type of shelter that provides safety.

Riza Bey - One of the persons who served as governor during the Ottoman Empire.

Roka (also called chicory) - A wild green plant that can be used in salads and other types of food.

Rudsack - A storage bag which is carried on one's back.

Scimitar - A sword used in battle which has a curved blade and broadens toward the point; a weapon that originated in Eastern countries.

Sheikh - An Arab chief, ruler or prince.

Strait - A waterway between two land masses.

Sultan - A Muslim King.

Tyranny - A government that oppresses its people.

Young Turks - Members of a revolutionary party in the Ottoman Empire who ousted the Sultan, Abdul Hamid II. Enver, Talaat and Djemal were the three Pashas or leaders of this movement who perpetuated the Armenian genocide.